A Cognitive-Behavioral Treatment Program for Overcoming Alcohol Problems

✓Treatments *That Work*™

A Cognitive-Behavioral Treatment Program for Overcoming Alcohol Problems

Workbook

Elizabeth E. Epstein • Barbara S. McCrady

OXFORD
UNIVERSITY PRESS

2009

OXFORD
UNIVERSITY PRESS

Oxford University Press, Inc., publishes works that further
Oxford University's objective of excellence
in research, scholarship, and education.

Oxford   New York
Auckland   Cape Town   Dar es Salaam   Hong Kong   Karachi
Kuala Lumpur   Madrid   Melbourne   Mexico City   Nairobi
New Delhi   Shanghai   Taipei   Toronto

With offices in
Argentina   Austria   Brazil   Chile   Czech Republic   France   Greece
Guatemala   Hungary   Italy   Japan   Poland   Portugal   Singapore
South Korea   Switzerland   Thailand   Turkey   Ukraine   Vietnam

Copyright © 2009 by Oxford University Press, Inc.

Published by Oxford University Press, Inc.
198 Madison Avenue, New York, New York 10016

www.oup.com

Oxford is a registered trademark of Oxford University Press

ISBN 978-0-19-532279-8

9 8 7 6 5 4 3 2 1

Printed in the United States of America
on acid-free paper

About Treatments *ThatWork*™

One of the most difficult problems confronting patients with various disorders and diseases is finding the best help available. Everyone is aware of friends or family who have sought treatment from a seemingly reputable practitioner, only to find out later from another doctor that the original diagnosis was wrong or the treatments recommended were inappropriate or perhaps even harmful. Most patients, or family members, address this problem by reading everything they can about their symptoms, seeking out information on the Internet, or aggressively "asking around" to tap knowledge from friends and acquaintances. Governments and healthcare policymakers are also aware that people in need don't always get the best treatments—something they refer to as "variability in healthcare practices."

Now healthcare systems around the world are attempting to correct this variability by introducing "evidence-based practice." This simply means that it is in everyone's interest that patients get the most up-to-date and effective care for a particular problem. Healthcare policymakers have also recognized that it is very useful to give consumers of healthcare as much information as possible, so that they can make intelligent decisions in a collaborative effort to improve health and mental health. This series, Treatments *ThatWork*™, is designed to accomplish just that. Only the latest and most effective interventions for particular problems are described in user-friendly language. To be included in this series, each treatment program must pass the highest standards of evidence available, as determined by a scientific advisory board. Thus, when individuals suffering from these problems or their family members seek out an expert clinician who is familiar with these interventions and decides that they are appropriate, they will have confidence that they are receiving the best care available. Of course, only your health care professional can decide on the right mix of treatments for you.

If you have problems with alcohol use, the program described in this workbook can help you overcome them. Through self-recording, you will identify your drinking patterns and triggers. You will learn to anticipate high-risk situations and plan for dealing with urges to drink. The program will incorporate additional skills that can help you remain abstinent, such as coping with anxiety and depression, building social support, being assertive, managing anger, and problem solving. Preparing for slips and relapses is also an important part of maintaining gains. This workbook provides information that will help you follow along with the program. It also includes worksheets for you to complete in session and at home. Working with a qualified mental health professional over 12 sessions, you can achieve the goal of abstinence from drinking.

David H. Barlow, Editor-in-Chief,
Treatments *ThatWork*™
Boston, MA

Contents

Chapter 1

Session 1: Introduction / Rationale / Self-Recording

Goals

- To learn about this program and what it will involve

- To commit to the program and sign a treatment contract

- To review the results of your pretreatment assessment

- To begin self-monitoring

- To talk about ways of achieving abstinence and develop an abstinence plan

- To plan how to deal with any upcoming high-risk situations in which you may be tempted to drink

The Journey Begins

Together in this therapy, we are starting a journey. The most successful and ambitious journeys all begin with a road map (a plan) and a destination (a goal). This therapy is part of the road map. The goal is sobriety. You will learn ways of quitting drinking and improving your life.

You will work together with your therapist to identify high-risk situations that may lead to drinking. Some of these situations will involve places, people, and things that you come across. Some of these situations will involve thoughts and emotions that are connected to your use. Some of these situations may come from your relationships. Your therapist will help you develop a plan and the skills to get through these tough situations. In each session, you will be introduced to a new skill or technique for dealing with high-risk situations.

The road will get bumpy at times. Sometimes things may be so rough that you will wonder if you've made a wrong turn. Many people who decide to quit drinking have a rough time in the beginning. Some people get discouraged by the tough times. Other people see these challenging times as a chance to learn more about themselves. Whatever happens, look at these rough times as chances to learn more about what kinds of situations are risky and what it takes to get through them.

When learning to ride a bicycle, most people will fall a few times. Most everyone gets back on the bicycle and eventually succeeds in learning to ride. You may go down the wrong path during this journey. If you do, recognizing this will be important so you can get back on the right road.

One very important part of this therapy is your commitment to working with your therapist. Each week you will be asked to do things outside of sessions. It is very important that you work hard at home. Work outside sessions is as important as work during sessions.

Many individuals have succeeded with this program. The things taught in this program help people stop drinking and build better lifestyles.

The Plan

Over the course of this program you will:

1. Study your drinking habits. Figure out what leads to drinking and what keeps it going.

2. Change habits and things around you that lead to or encourage drinking.

3. Learn positive alternatives to drinking alcohol.

Your therapist will help you through these phases during the next 12 weeks. In the first three sessions, the focus will be on phase one. As part of phase one, you will look at what people, places, and things lead to drinking. You will also look at what happens because of drinking.

The following is a list of some important points about the treatment program you are about to begin.

■ People with problems similar to yours have learned to stop drinking.

■ Drinking is something you have learned to do. Habits can be changed. Right now, it does not matter how the drinking got started; it is important to figure out how to change.

■ The goal is to be totally abstinent—to stop drinking altogether. Drinking should stop early on in the treatment. Sometimes people will have slips, but successful people learn from mistakes and get back with the program.

■ Work in between sessions is as important as work during sessions. There will be things that you will be asked to do to learn and practice new skills. Practice is the only way to get this right. Often it is not possible to learn everything well during the session. If you do not complete the tasks required, your therapist reserves the right to reschedule your session in order to give you an opportunity to make up the work.

Treatment Contract

It is important that you commit to this program and agree to complete the tasks that are required of you in order to get the most benefit from treatment. Please read and sign the following brief treatment contract.

1. I understand that this treatment will include 12 sessions over 3 months, and I agree to participate for that length of time. If I want to withdraw from the program, I agree to discuss this decision with my therapist prior to taking this action.

2. I agree to attend all sessions and to be prompt. If it is absolutely necessary that I cancel a session, I will call at least 24 hours in advance to reschedule. I also agree to call in advance if I will be late to a session.

3. I understand that this treatment is intended for people who want to abstain from alcohol. I understand that I must work on remaining clean and sober.

4. I agree that it is essential for me to come to the session alcohol-free. I understand that I will be asked to leave any session to which I come with a blood alcohol level (BAL) of over .05. I will be required to arrange safe transportation home.

5. I understand that I will be given a breath test for alcohol use each session.

6. I understand that I will be expected to practice some of the skills I discuss in treatment. I agree to bring in the workbook with the completed homework each week to discuss with my therapist.

7. I understand that I will be expected to attend all scheduled weekly sessions as research has shown that this type of treatment is effective only if clients attend scheduled appointments on a regular basis.

I have reviewed the above statements with my therapist and I agree to abide by them.

_____   _____

Client   Date

_____   _____

Therapist   Date

4

Prior to starting treatment, you completed an intake assessment where you filled out self-reports and questionnaires. These measures help your therapist better understand your drinking problem and provide vital information your therapist can use to tailor the treatment program to fit your needs. You may have also been advised to visit your physician for a medical check-up. Since alcohol is a toxin and heavy drinking can affect your liver and other vital organs, it is a good idea to see your general practitioner to assess your health. Ask your doctor to perform the following tests and bring the lab results in to share with your therapist.

■ Gamma glutamic transpeptidase (GGTP)

■ Aspartate aminotransferase (AST)

■ Alanine aminotransferase (ALT)

■ Mean corpuscular volume (MCV)

■ Bilirubin

■ Uric acid

After covering the introductory material in the first session, your therapist will review with you the results of the pretreatment assessment. He or she will work with you to complete a Feedback Sheet. Your therapist may provide you with data and have you fill out the sheet on your own. A blank sheet for your use is provided on page 6. Alternatively, your therapist may complete the sheet for you.

Feedback Sheet

1. Based on the information I obtained during the assessment, I calculated the number of "standard drinks" you consumed in a typical week during the last 3 months before you came in:

     Total number of standard drinks per *week* _____

     Average number of standard drinks per *drinking day* _____

2. When we look at everyone who drinks in the United States, you have been drinking more than approximately _____ percent of the population in the country.

3. I also estimated your highest and average blood alcohol level (BAL) in the past 3 months. Your BAL is based on how many standard drinks you consume, the length of time over which you drink that much, whether you are a man or a woman, and how much you weigh. So,

     Your estimated *peak BAL* in the past 3 months was _____

     Your estimated *typical BAL* in an average week was _____

4. You have experienced many negative consequences from drinking. Here are some of the most important:

     _____   _____

     _____   _____

     _____   _____

Alcohol Information

Before reviewing the results of your assessment with your therapist, you should familiarize yourself with Tables 1.1–1.4, which provide information about alcohol and alcohol use. Your therapist will review this information with you in session.

Table 1.1 Alcohol Information

Beer

Ounces	Standard drinks			
	Light	Regular	European	Ice
12	.75	1	1.25	1.5
16	1	1.33	1.66	—

Wine 5 ounces = 1 standard drink

Amount	Ounces	Standard Drinks
750 ml	25.6	5
1.5 L	51	10

Hard Liquor

1.5 ounces of 80 proof liquor = 1 standard drink

Liquor			Equivalent number of standard drinks		
Amount	Street Name	Ounces	80 proof	100 proof	190 proof
	"Shot"	1.5	1	1.25	2.38
200 ml	"Half pint"	6.8	4.5	5.67	10.77
375 ml	"Pint"	12.75	8.5	10.63	20.19
750 ml	"Fifth"	25.5	17	21.25	40.38
1.75 L	"Half Gallon"	59.5	40	49.58	94.21

Table 1.2 Blood Alcohol Level Estimation Charts

Men

Approximate Blood Alcohol Percentage

Drinks	Body Weight in Pounds								Sample Behavioral Effects
	100	120	140	160	180	200	220	240	
0	.00	.00	.00	.00	.00	.00	.00	.00	Only completely safe limit
1	.04	.03	.03	.02	.02	.02	.02	.02	Impairment begins
2	.08	.06	.05	.05	.04	.04	.03	.03	Driving skills significantly affected; Information processing altered
3	.11	.09	.08	.07	.06	.06	.05	.05	
4	.15	.12	.11	.09	.08	.08	.07	.06	
5	.19	.16	.13	.12	.11	.09	.09	.08	
6	.23	.19	.16	.14	.13	.11	.10	.09	Legally intoxicated; Criminal penalties; Reaction time slowed; Loss of balance; Impaired movement; Slurred speech
7	.26	.22	.19	.16	.15	.13	.12	.11	
8	.30	.25	.21	.19	.17	.15	.14	.13	
9	.34	.28	.24	.21	.19	.17	.15	.14	
10	.38	.31	.27	.23	.21	.19	.17	.16	

One drink is 1.5 oz. shot of hard liquor, 12 oz. of beer, or 5 oz. of table wine.

Women

Approximate Blood Alcohol Percentage

Drinks	Body Weight in Pounds									Sample Behavioral Effects
	90	100	120	140	160	180	200	220	240	
0	.00	.00	.00	.00	.00	.00	.00	.00	.00	Only completely safe limit
1	.05	.05	.04	.03	.03	.03	.02	.02	.02	Impairment begins
2	.10	.09	.08	.07	.06	.05	.05	.04	.04	Driving skills significantly affected; Information processing altered
3	.15	.14	.11	.10	.09	.08	.07	.06	.06	
4	.20	.18	.15	.13	.11	.10	.09	.08	.08	
5	.25	.23	.19	.16	.14	.13	.11	.10	.09	
6	.30	.27	.23	.19	.17	.15	.14	.12	.11	Legally intoxicated; Criminal penalties; Reaction time slowed; Loss of balance; Impaired movement; Slurred speech
7	.35	.32	.27	.23	.20	.18	.16	.14	.13	
8	.40	.36	.30	.26	.23	.20	.18	.17	.15	
9	.45	.41	.34	.29	.26	.23	.20	.19	.17	
10	.51	.45	.38	.32	.28	.25	.23	.21	.19	

One drink is 1.5 oz. shot of hard liquor, 12 oz. of beer or 5 oz. of table wine.

Subtract .015 for each hour that you take to consume the number of drinks listed in the table. For example, if you are a 160 pound woman and have two drinks in two hours, your BAC would be $.06 - (2 \times .015) = .03$

NOTE: Blood Alcohol Level (BAL) charts do not take into consideration a wide range of additional variables that contribute to the determination of BAL's achieved and the behavioral effects experienced at a given BAL. These additional variables include: age, water-to-body-mass ratio, ethanol metabolism, tolerance level, drugs or medications taken, amount and type of food in the stomach during consumption, speed of consumption, and general physical condition. Thus, BAL charts only provide extremely rough estimates and should never be used alone to determine any individual's safe level of drinking.
Adapted from BAC Charts produced by the National Clearinghouse for Alcohol and Drug Information.

Table 1.3 Percentile Table for Alcohol Use

Drinks per week	Total	Men	Women
0	35	29	41
1	58	46	68
2	66	54	77
3	68	57	78
4	71	61	82
5	77	67	86
6	78	68	87
7	80	70	89
8	81	71	89
9	82	73	90
10	83	75	91
11	84	75	91
12	85	77	92
13	86	77	93
14	87	79	94
15	87	80	94
16	88	81	94
17	89	82	95
18	90	84	96
19	91	85	96
20	91	86	96
21	92	88	96
22	92	88	97
23–24	93	88	97
25	93	89	98
26–27	94	89	98
28	94	90	98
29	95	91	98
30–33	95	92	98
34–35	95	93	98
36	96	93	98
37–39	96	94	98
40	96	94	99
41–46	97	95	99
47–48	97	96	99
49–50	98	97	99
51–62	98	97	99
63–64	99	97	>99.5
65–84	99	98	>99.6
85–101	99	99	>99.9
102–159	>99.5	99	>99.9
160+	>99.8	>99.5	>99.9

Source: 1990 National Alcohol Survey, Alcohol Research Group, Berkeley. Courtesy of Dr. Robin Room.

Table 1.4 Common Effects of Different Levels of Intoxication

.02–.06%	This is the "normal" social drinking range. Driving, even at these levels, is unsafe.
.08%	Memory, judgment, and perception are impaired. Legally intoxicated in most states.
.1%	Reaction time and coordination of movement are affected. Legally intoxicated in all states.
.15%	Vomiting may occur in normal drinkers; balance is often impaired.
.2%	Memory "blackout" may occur, causing loss of recall for events occurring while intoxicated.
.3%	Unconsciousness in a normal person, though some remain conscious at levels in excess of .6% if tolerance is very high.
.4–.5%	Fatal dose for a normal person, though some survive higher levels if tolerance is very high.

Self-Monitoring

An important part of treatment is to work with facts and accurate information. In your case, your therapist will want to learn about what happens during your day.

The best way to collect facts is to write them down as they happen. Trying to recall things later is difficult. Everyone makes mistakes when they try to figure out what happened in the past, whether it was a few days ago or yesterday.

Self-monitoring is when you write down what you do during the day as it relates to your drinking. By recording your drinking and urges, your therapist will get a better idea of what is going on. Monitoring will help you and your therapist identify patterns in your life. Your monitoring records will help you realize the behavior chains that lead to drinking.

With self-monitoring, drinkers are surprised by how much they are drinking and that their drinking falls into patterns that happen over and over. Self-monitoring also helps you realize how often you are getting urges or desires to drink and what leads to these urges. Overall, self-monitoring will help your therapist assess your progress over the duration of the program.

On the self-recording cards provided in the appendix at the end of the book, write down your urges to drink and any drinks you may have had. You will need to do this on a daily basis. The appendix contains enough recording cards for two weeks. Please feel free to make photocopies as you will need additional cards as treatment progresses.

Your therapist can help you come up with a reminder system so that you remember to monitor your drinking every day. You may wish to keep your recording cards in a visible location in your home, like on your bedside table or near the front door. When you have a drink or experience an urge, be sure to write it down as soon as possible. Don't rely on your memory later.

Figure 1.1 shows an example of a completed self-monitoring card. Review this sample along with the instructions for completing the card together with your therapist. Because self-monitoring is so important, it is essential that you understand exactly how it should be done. If you have questions, talk to your therapist.

Instructions for Self-Monitoring

The self-monitoring cards are an easy way to keep track of what is happening to your urges and drinking from day to day. Complete a card every day using the following instructions.

Date: Make sure to write in the date that you are filling in the card. You should fill in a card for every day of the week. The information from your cards will be used to identify patterns that emerge during the week.

Urges: In the section marked "Urges," write down the time the urge occurred and how intense it was. For intensity, put down a number between one and seven to describe how strong the urge was. Number 1 would mean that the urge was very weak. Number 7 would mean that the urge was one of the strongest that you have ever felt. If the urge was somewhere in the middle, then give it a number in between. Write down what triggered the urge.

Drinks: In the "Drinks" section, record information about what you drank, how much, and the amount of alcohol in the drink.

In the column labeled "Time," write down the time you started drinking.

Self-Monitoring Card

Daily monitoring

Date _10/8/08_

Urges

Time	How strong? (1–7)	Trigger
8:00 a.m.	4	Traffic during commute
5:30 p.m.	7	Irritated when I came home

Drinks

Time	Type of drink	Amount (in ounces)	% Alcohol	Trigger
6:00 p.m.	Wine	1 bottle 25 oz.	12%	Fight with John

Figure 1.1

Example of Completed Self-Recording Card

In the column labeled "Type of Drink," write down the name of the drink you had (e.g., red wine, light beer, or martini)

In the column labeled "Amount," write down how many drinks you had and the number of ounces for each drink. For example, the person who completed the sample recording card in Figure 1.1 says she drank a 750-ml bottle (a "fifth"). A 750-ml bottle has about 25 ounces of liquid. Maybe in your case, you would have had a drink with vodka in it. If so, you should estimate the amount of vodka in your cocktail. One way to do this is to know the size of the glass and how much liquid it holds. It is helpful to measure your drinks, so you can understand how much you're drinking.

In the column labeled "% Alcohol," write down the alcohol content of the drink you are having. Most times, this information can be found on the bottle or can.

In the column labeled "Trigger," list the event that led to the drinking.

Abstinence

The first phase in treatment is helping you to actually stop drinking. Then, you will move on to learning skills to stay sober, prevent relapse, cope better with problems, etc.

There are several options for stopping your use of alcohol. Your therapist will review with you the following options:

1. inpatient detoxification

2. outpatient detoxification

3. going "cold turkey"

4. stopping on your own, with the help of the therapist

After discussing these options with your therapist, you will work together to devise a plan for achieving abstinence. Record your ideas in the space provided.

Abstinence Plan

At the end of each session, you will spend some time discussing with your therapist any problem situations that you think might come up in the following week. As you progress through therapy, you will get better and better at anticipating and handling these. A "high-risk situation" is a situation in which you would find it very difficult not to drink.

Work with your therapist to identify at least one high-risk situation coming up in the next week. Write down ideas about how to handle this situation on the High-Risk Situations worksheet. Use the back of your self-recording cards to record how you actually handled the anticipated situation, and write down any unexpected high-risk situations that may have arisen during the week.

Example of Completed High-Risk Situations Worksheet

What high-risk situations do you think you may experience this week?

Situation 1: *Friday—end of the work week—will want a reward for working hard*

How can you handle this situation?

- Tell myself that being sober is a gift

- Go to the gym instead of the bar

- Take a bubble bath and read new book I buy

Situation 2: *Have to get child support payment to my ex-wife*

How can you handle this situation?

- Put the check in her mailbox when she's not home

- Get a pizza after I drop off the check and bring it home to eat

- Ask my brother to drop off the check for me

Situation 3: *Neighbors' son's sweet 16 at a dance hall*

How can you handle this situation?

- Skip cocktail hour and arrive for dinner

- Eat something as soon as I sit down at table and ask wife to get me a soda

- Put my hand over my wine glass when waiter comes by with wine and then put my wine glass on another table

High-Risk Situations

What high-risk situations do you think you may experience this week?

Situation 1:
How can you handle this situation?

a.

b.

c.

d.

Situation 2:
How can you handle this situation?

a.

b.

c.

d.

Situation 3:
How can you handle this situation?

a.

b.

c.

d.

Situation 4:
How can you handle this situation?

a.

b.

c.

d.

Homework

✎ If not done already, make an appointment with your physician to have a physical and get blood tests to check liver function.

✎ Begin self-monitoring your alcohol use and urges (intensity, frequency) using the self-recording cards in the appendix.

✎ Use the back of your self-recording cards to record any high-risk situations you encounter during the week and how you handled them.

✎ Review the information in this chapter.

✎ Complete the Drinking Patterns Questionnaire (DPQ). Your therapist will distribute this questionnaire to you at the end of Session 1.

Chapter 2   *Session 2: Functional Analysis*

Goals

- To begin tracking your progress
- To analyze the chain of events that maintains your drinking

Graphing Progress

Together with your therapist, you will use the information from your completed self-recording cards to complete the Alcohol Use and Urges Graph. On this graph, you will record the following information each week:

1. Total number of standard drinks you consumed for the week (add up the number of drinks)

2. Total number of urges to drink you experienced during the week (urge frequency) (count up the number of urges)

3. Average strength of your urges during the week (1–7) (add up the ratings for all the urges during the week and divide by the total number of urges)

You will update and review this graph at the beginning of each session with your therapist.

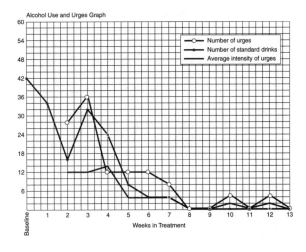

Alcohol Use and Urges Graph

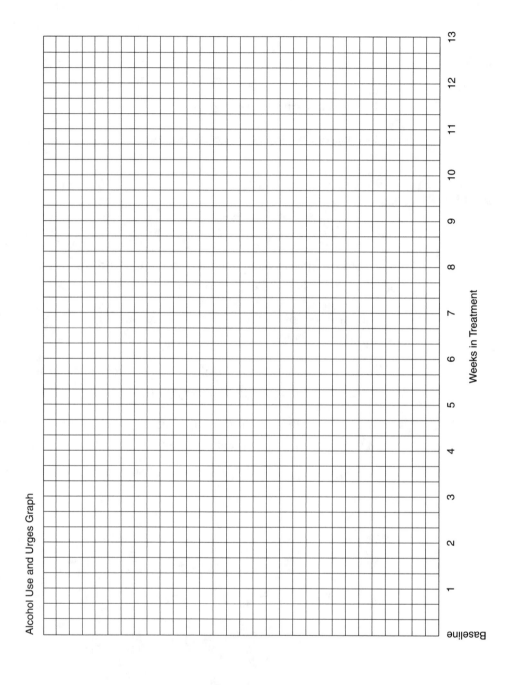

Baseline   1   2   3   4   5   6   7   8   9   10   11   12   13

Weeks in Treatment

Functional Analysis

The first step in achieving abstinence is to understand more about your drinking. Together with your therapist, you will carefully identify and analyze all the factors that seem to be high-risk situations for you to drink. Then, you will put it all together to come up with a plan that will work for you. This is called a **functional analysis** or a habit analysis.

A functional analysis is a very important part of this treatment. It means looking at what happens before and after you drink. This helps us learn about the chains of events that keep your drinking going. Everyone has his own special type of behavior chain, but every chain can be looked at using the model shown in Figure 2.1.

Every behavior chain follows a pattern: Triggers lead to thoughts and feelings that set up the drinker. After drinking, some good things happen (positive consequences) immediately and bad things (negative consequences) come later. Let's look at each step of the behavior chain (see Table 2.1).

Figure 2.1

Drinking Behavior Chain

Table 2.1 Steps to Functional Analysis

Triggers	People, places, and things will be associated with drinking. A trigger is something that usually occurs before drinking. A trigger can be something easy to see or something sneaky. Often the drinker is not aware of the triggers. Triggers don't make people drink; they just set up thoughts and feelings connected to drinking.
Thoughts and feelings	Triggers set up thoughts and feelings. The triggers bring up feelings and ideas that are connected to drinking. These thoughts and feelings can be nice or unpleasant. Some examples are "I need to drink to be more sociable," "People will think I am weak if I don't drink," "Drinking will help me relax," or "Drinking will make me happy."
Drink	Drinking is something you do. It is a behavior that is a part of the chain.
Positive consequences	Very often something nice happens when someone drinks. The alcohol will often cause pleasant feelings. People learn to expect that alcohol will make them more relaxed, more sociable, or happy. These pleasant effects help keep people stuck on alcohol.
Negative consequences	The trouble that comes with alcohol often comes later. The trouble comes in many forms: arguments in the family, problems with a boss, financial difficulties, poor health, etc. Because the trouble comes later on, many people don't always make the connection between the trouble and their drinking. Many times, the possible trouble is out of your mind when thoughts of the pleasant parts of drinking are on your mind.

The first part of therapy is to conduct a functional analysis of what gets and keeps you drinking. Let's find out about your triggers. Later, you will learn new ways to break the chains.

The How-To's of Functional Analysis

Doing a functional analysis is just going back and figuring out the details of what happened when you drank. Start with one example, maybe the last time you drank, and look at the pattern or chain of events. Sample behavior chains are shown in Figures 2.2 and 2.3.

Trigger	Thoughts and feelings	Response	Positive consequences	Negative consequences
Friday 5 p.m., invitation from coworkers to go to sports bar	Tired and tense. "I deserve a break. I'll just have one quick drink and go home"	At sports bar Friday evening—stayed 2 1/2 hours, had 4 drinks instead of 1. Drank 4/16 ounce bud ice, or 7.5 standard drinks over 2 hours.	Relaxation, initial euphoria from alcohol, socialize with friends, fun	Stayed too long, drank too much, spouse angry (argument followed), didn't see kids, drove under influence, had a hangover the next day

Figure 2.2

Example 1 of Completed Behavior Chain

Trigger	Thoughts and feelings	Response	Positive consequences	Negative consequences
Home from work—house is a mess, laundry piled up, time to cook dinner.	How in the world am I going to get everything done? I'm tired. This isn't fair. I'll have a glass of wine to calm down. Tired, angry, overwhelmed.	Have 8 oz. glass of wine with ice. Then have 2 more. (24 ounces total = about 5 standard drinks)	Relaxed. Not angry anymore. Don't care temporarily.	Fell asleep. No dinner made, house still a mess. Husband angry, kids neglected. Work piling up, no resolution to problem. Hangover next morning. Call in sick.

Figure 2.3

Example 2 of Completed Behavior Chain

1. First you write in the "Drink" column when and where the drinking happened. In Example 1, the person had five standard drinks at the sports bar Friday evening between 5:30 p.m. and 8:30 p.m. for a BAL of .075.

2. Then think back to what happened before the drinking happened. What were the people, places, or things that set up the drinking? Write these things in the "Trigger" column. In this example, the person had had a tough week and coworkers invited him out to a sports bar. Friday at 5 p.m. was also a trigger.

3. After writing the triggers, think back to those thoughts and feelings that made drinking more likely. In this example, the person thinks about being tired and tense after the work week, feels he deserves a break, and anticipates relaxation and fun at the bar. He thinks, "I will have a beer."

4. After this, think about what happened after drinking. Remember the good things, the positive consequences. It is realistic to say that good things will happen, in the short term, to people when they drink. In our example, the person feels more relaxed, enjoys the initial euphoria from the alcohol, and enjoys socializing with his friends from work.

5. Now think about the things that happened later: the negative consequences. The problems created by drinking often come later on. In this example, the person had an argument with his wife, missed seeing his kids before bedtime, his driving was impaired, he risked getting a DUI, and he had a hangover the next day.

As with most people, the person in this example falls into a pattern. Some triggers will set off thoughts and emotions that lead to drinking. The drinking leads to some nice things happening. These nice things encourage the drinker to keep using alcohol.

The functional analysis helps us learn about patterns. Most people are not aware of the patterns and habits that happen in their lives, and it takes some detective work to identify these patterns.

The first step in doing behavior chains is to identifying your own personal set of triggers, which can be categorized into environmental, interpersonal, emotions/thoughts, and physical. See Figure 2.4 for a sample list of triggers.

Now it is your turn. To start, record your triggers in the space provided.

List of Triggers

Environmental (places, things)	5 p.m. on weeknight, preparing dinner at home
	Saturday evening
	Restaurant
	Messy house
	Dinner party or barbecue
	10 p.m., home
	Working in yard on hot day
Interpersonal (people)	Eating out with spouse
	Night out with friends
	5:00 on Friday and office buddies going to happy hour after work
	When my mother is bossy
	Argument with partner
	Kids are loud and boisterous
	Boss criticizing me at a meeting
Emotions/Thoughts	Anxiety
	Depression, sadness
	Anger, frustration
	Loneliness
	Stressed out, tense
Physical	Back pain
	Headache
	Can't sleep

Figure 2.4

Example of Completed List of Triggers

List of Triggers

Environmental (places, things)

_____

_____

_____

Interpersonal (people)

_____

_____

_____

Emotions/Thoughts

_____

_____

_____

Physical

_____

_____

_____

After you have stated your list of triggers, work with your therapist to complete two behavior chains on the Behavior Chain worksheet (blank copies at end of chapter).

High-Risk Situations for the Week

Work with your therapist to identify at least one high-risk situation coming up in the next week. Write down ideas about how to handle this situation on the High-Risk Situations worksheet. Use the back of your self-recording card to record how you actually handled the anticipated situation, and write down any unexpected high-risk situations that may have come up during the week.

High-Risk Situations

What high-risk situations do you think you may experience this week?

Situation 1:
How can you handle this situation?

a. _____

b. _____

c. _____

d. _____

Situation 2:
How can you handle this situation?

a. _____

b. _____

c. _____

d. _____

Situation 3:
How can you handle this situation?

a. _____

b. _____

c. _____

d. _____

Situation 4:
How can you handle this situation?

a. _____

b. _____

c. _____

d. _____

Homework

✎ Continue self-recording. Remember to use the back of your self-recording cards to write down the ways you handled your high-risk situations for the week.

✎ If not completed in session, finish filling out your list of triggers.

✎ Complete two or more behavior chains in detail. Blank copies of the Behavior Chain worksheet can be found at the end of the chapter.

✎ Review the information in this chapter.

Behavior Chain

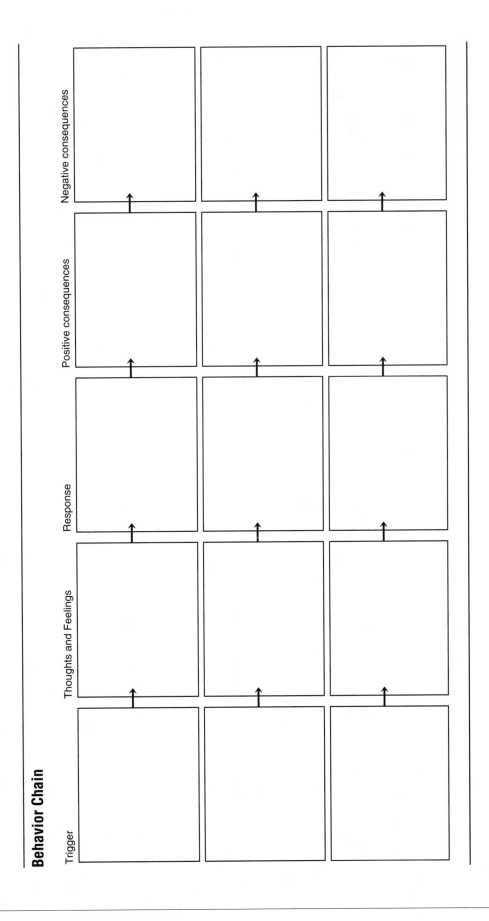

Trigger → Thoughts and Feelings → Response → Positive consequences → Negative consequences

Behavior Chain

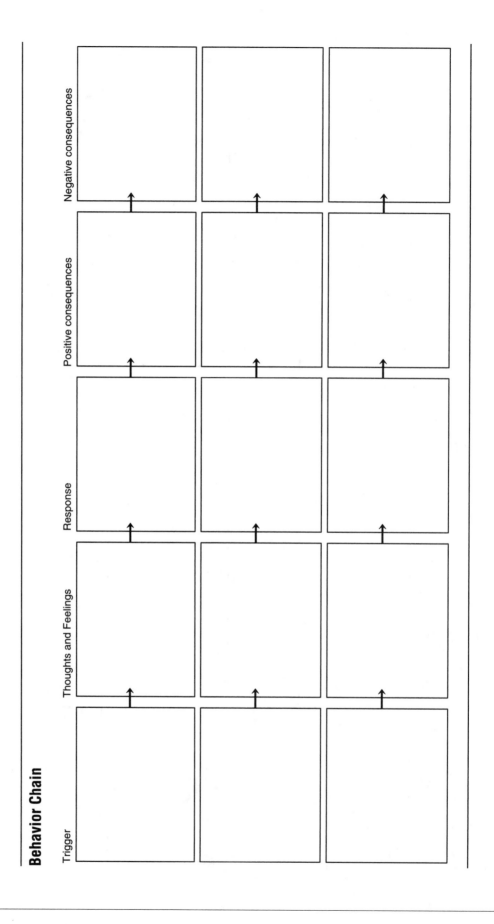

Behavior Chain

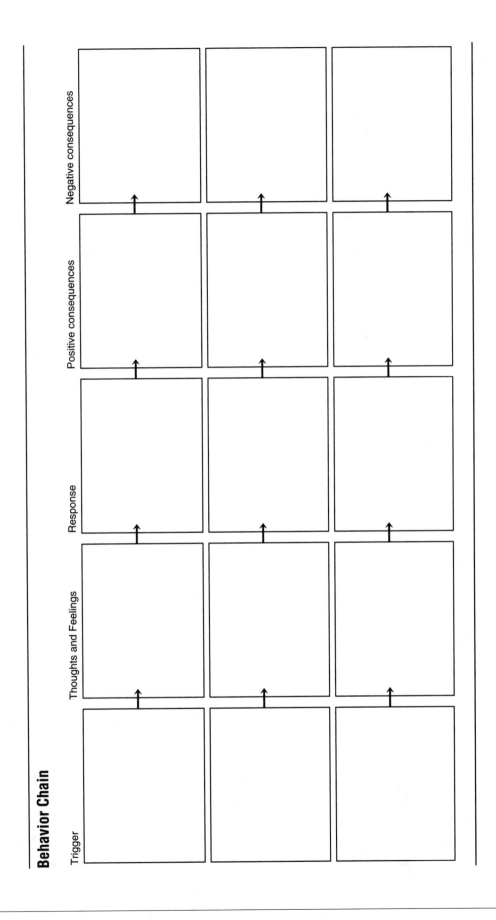

Trigger → Thoughts and Feelings → Response → Positive consequences → Negative consequences

Behavior Chain

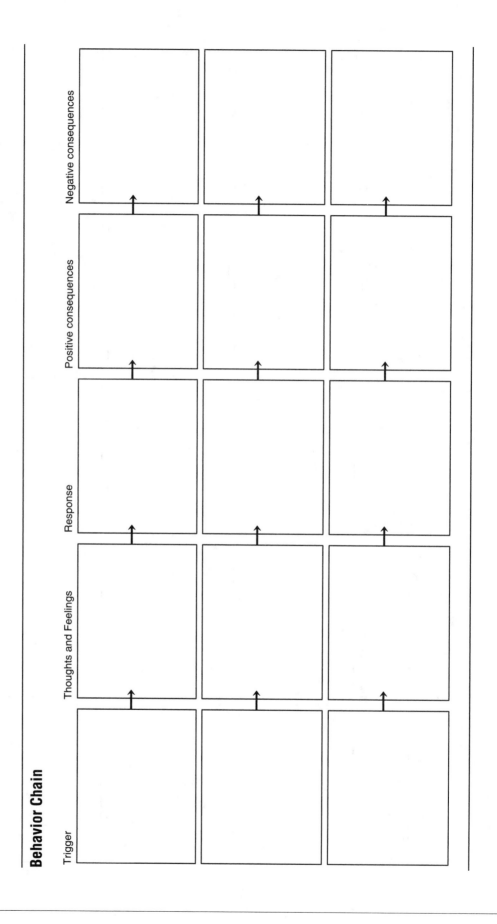

Session 3: High-Risk Hierarchy / Social Network Triggers / Self-Management Plans

Goals

- To identify your high-risk situations and list them in order of difficulty

- To identify heavy drinkers in your social network

- To develop a plan for dealing with the triggers for your drinking

Graphing Progress

In session, you will review the week with your therapist and together update your Alcohol Use and Urges Graph in Chapter 2 using the information from your most recently completed self-recording cards.

Looking Ahead for Trouble

Last week, you identified some of the major situations, feelings, people, and behaviors that are associated with your drinking. This week, your therapist is going to help you plan for these difficulties.

Smart travelers look ahead for possible trouble. By looking ahead for rough spots in the road, they can handle tough situations better. Travelers who see the trouble ahead on the road can make changes to steer around the problem. In the same way, people who quit drinking can look ahead for difficult situations. Smart people plan for the rough spots.

Everybody who has stopped drinking has faced people, places, or things that made it difficult to stay sober. Some situations are more difficult than others. For you, some situations will be easier to handle. Other situations will be more difficult to manage. What are your rough spots? What people, places, emotions, or things can be trouble for you? What are your triggers for drinking? You made a list of these triggers last week. Look back to Chapter 2 for your list, and add anything new that you noticed this week. Think of what goes with drinking:

- People

- Places

- Things you see, like bottles

- Problems with your partner

- Emotions, like sadness, anger, boredom, and happiness

- Problems with your children

- Good times

- Events, like parties

Some rough spots are harder and others are easier to handle. You can usually tell ahead of time how hard something will be. By thinking about how hard different situations can be, you can be ready for the tougher ones.

Now go back to your list of triggers from Chapter 2. Add any new triggers to the list as necessary. For each trigger listed, think about how easy or difficult it would be to avoid drinking when that particular trigger comes up. Arrange your triggers from the hardest to the easiest on the High-Risk Hierarchy worksheet provided.

Then, rate how hard each situation is for you. The easiest way to do this is by using numbers. Use numbers between 0 and 100 to describe each situation. Larger numbers mean that the situation is harder to handle. Smaller numbers mean that the situation is easier. Something that is no trouble at all would get a number 0. Something that would be very hard for you to handle would get a higher number. A rating of 100 would mean that the situation was the most difficult one for you to handle without drinking. Figure 3.1 shows a sample High-Risk Hierarchy.

Now it is your turn to create a hierarchy. Use the following worksheet to put your high-risk situations in order from hardest to easiest.

High-Risk Hierarchy

Difficult Situation	How Hard?	
	very easy	very hard
	0 - - - - - - - 100	
1. Being angry after an argument with my partner	95	
2. Being at a party with alcohol	85	
3. Working on the yard	85	
4. Co-workers going out for drinks invite me	80	
5. My partner yelling at me for drinking	75	
6. Being at a professional meeting	65	
7. Watching TV	55	

Figure 3.1
Example of Completed High-Risk Hierarchy

High-Risk Hierarchy

very easy   very hard

0 - - - - - - 100

Difficult Situation

Who's in Your Circle? Who's in Your Corner?

What Is a Social Network?

A social network is your "social circle"—people who are important to you, people who you spend most of your time with, people you care about most, people who care about you. It can include spouses, children, parents, siblings, other relatives, friends, coworkers, etc.

What Does A Social Network Have to Do With Drinking?

We hear things like, "Everyone I know drinks. I drink less than most people I know!" That's because people who drink tend to socialize with others who drink. That can make it seem "normal" to drink frequently or heavily. Maybe 80% of the people you know drink frequently, but you are all among a small percentage of people in the United States. Overall, most people don't drink that much. See the facts for women and men included in this chapter.

Who's in Your Circle? Who's in Your Corner?

Facts for Women

fact: Social networks are extremely important to women. Men tend to think in terms of hierarchies (who has more power), while women tend to think in circles (who is in my inner circle of friends; who is more distant).

fact: Among women in the United States in 1990, 41% didn't drink at all. As a woman, if you drink more than 1 drink per week, you're drinking more than 68% of the women in the United States—that is, only 32% of women in the United States drink more than one drink per week. Only 23% of women in the United States drink more than 2 drinks per week.

fact: Among 102 female problem drinkers, the average number of drinkers in their social networks was 6, or almost three-quarters of their social networks.

fact: Among those 102 female problem drinkers, the more drinkers in the social network and the more heavy drinkers in the social network, the more often the woman drank herself.

fact: Among female problem drinkers, approximately 42% reported that their spouses were moderate or heavy drinkers; 29% of their male partners had a current or lifetime drinking problem.

fact: Emotional situations and social situations are among the strongest drinking triggers for women.

fact: Heavy drinking spouses can serve as an interpersonal trigger for women to drink.

Who's in Your Circle? Who's in Your Corner?

Facts for Men

fact: Social networks are extremely important to men. Men have a higher proportion of drinkers in their social networks than women.

fact: Among men in the United States in 1990, 29% didn't drink at all. If you drink more 1 drink per week, you're drinking more than 46% of the men in the United States—that is, only 54% of men in the United States drink more than one drink per week. Only 33% of men in the United States drink more than 4 drinks per week.

fact: Among men with drinking problems, many of their closest and most important friends are drinkers.

fact: Having more people in the social network who support continued drinking predicts a poorer outcome, but finding more people who support abstinence is associated with treatment success.

fact: Environmental situations and work-related stress are among the strongest drinking triggers for men.

fact: Social pressure to drink and interpersonal conflicts may be triggers for relapse.

What Does Your Social Network Have to Do With Your Drinking?

This is up to you. Do you want to decide when and how much you drink, or do you want other people to decide? If you learn to manage drinking triggers related to heavy drinkers in your social network, you will be able to decide for yourself!

Exercise—Your Social Network

Turn to the Your Social Network worksheet (see Figure 3.2 for a completed example). You see there are circles within circles. Put your name in the middle. Write the name(s) of the person or people you consider closest to you in the inner circle, and then move out from there in terms of placement. So the people in the outermost circle would be less close to you than those in the inner circles. This is a picture of your social network.

Your Social Network

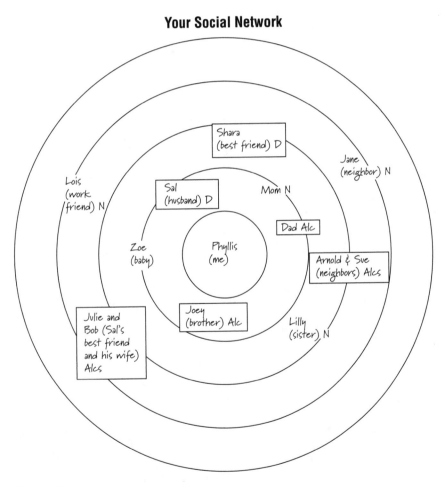

Figure 3.2

Example of Completed Your Social Network Worksheet

Draw a box around those who drink at all. Put a "D," for Heavy Drinker, next to names of people who you think are heavy drinkers. Put an "Alc" (for alcohol problem) next to names of people you think have an alcohol problem. Put an "N" next to people in the network who are nondrinkers.

Exercise—Dealing With Heavy Drinkers in Your Social Network

Next, complete the Dealing With Heavy Drinkers in Your Social Network worksheet (see Figure 3.3 for a completed example). List the people in your social network who might be considered "interpersonal triggers" for you to drink, along with a sentence or two about how their drinking may impact your efforts to stay sober.

Dealing With Heavy Drinkers in Your Social Network

Name of heavy drinker _Sal_

How might this person's drinking affect your efforts to stop drinking and stay sober?

1. Sal keeps vodka in the house and that's a temptation for me.

2. We have a nightcap together—I will miss that.

3. When we socialize we usually drink.

Name of heavy drinker _Dad_

How might this person's drinking affect your efforts to stop drinking and stay sober?

1. Dad keeps telling me I don't have a problem and that is nonsense.

2. When Dad and Mom come over he expects to be served drinks.

Name of heavy drinker _Shara_

How might this person's drinking affect your efforts to stop drinking and stay sober?

1. I love Shara but we usually do drink when we get together. We drink and giggle, and that's so much fun.

Name of heavy drinker

How might this person's drinking affect your efforts to stop drinking and stay sober?

Figure 3.3

Example of Completed Heavy Drinkers in Your Social Network Worksheet

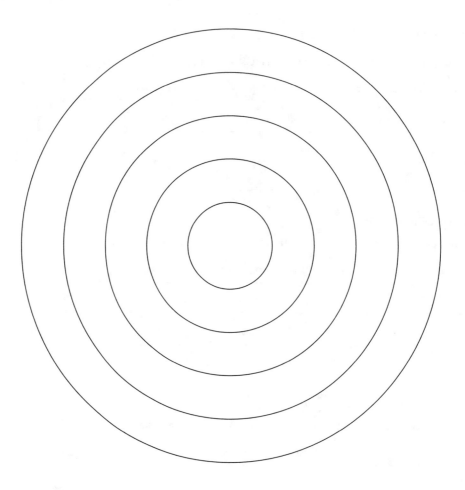

Dealing With Heavy Drinkers in Your Social Network

Name of heavy drinker_____

How might this person's drinking affect your efforts to stop drinking and stay sober?

_____

_____

_____

_____

Name of heavy drinker_____

How might this person's drinking affect your efforts to stop drinking and stay sober?

_____

_____

_____

_____

Name of heavy drinker_____

How might this person's drinking affect your efforts to stop drinking and stay sober?

_____

_____

_____

_____

Name of heavy drinker_____

How might this person's drinking affect your efforts to stop drinking and stay sober?

_____

_____

_____

_____

In this program, you have spent some time talking about your triggers. Triggers come in all shapes and sizes. Some lead to very strong urges, while others lead to very difficult situations. Some are easier to handle than others. Some involve loved ones; others come from your daily routine.

- Knowing about triggers is not enough. You need a plan!

- Developing a good plan takes patience and a lot of thinking. This program will teach you a step-by-step method that makes planning much easier.

- There are both your personal triggers and other triggers related to your relationships.

Follow these steps for designing a plan for managing your triggers:

1. Pick out triggers that you will come across soon. Start with an easier trigger. As you get more practice at this, you can plan for harder triggers.

2. Write down as many ideas as possible for handling the trigger. Be creative and brainstorm! Do not worry about being silly or unrealistic. The best ideas often come when you let ideas fly without stopping to think about what is good or bad about each one. The evaluation will come later. There are three kinds of strategies for handling triggers:

   - Remove yourself from the situation to avoid trouble.
   - Change things around you to avoid the trigger. For example, get rid of alcohol around the house or do not walk past the liquor store.
   - Think or act in a different way when you are faced with the trigger. For example, someone may avoid drinking by remembering the consequences that will come later.

3. *After* coming up with several ideas, think about them all and write down what is good and bad about each one. Now is the time to think about what you need to do for each one of the ideas. Remember, some consequences of your plan will happen quickly and others will happen later. Try to think them through. The goal here is to think about the pros and cons of each idea.

4. Think about how easy or hard each idea would be to carry out instead of drinking. Some will be hard to do, others will be easy. For each idea or plan, give it a number between 1 and 10 that shows how hard it would be to do

compared to just drinking in response to that trigger. For example, the easiest plan that you can do would get a 1, and the hardest would get a 10. Write down how hard each idea would be for you. That is, how difficult would it be to carry out the new plan in place of old behavior that involved drinking in response to the same trigger?

5. Pick a plan. Choose the plan or plans that have the best balance between positive and negative consequences. Try to pick ones that will not be too hard for you.

6. After putting a plan to work, check to see how it is working. If a plan is not working, do not be afraid to make changes or to pick another idea.

Now it's your turn. Use the Self-Management Planning Sheet to write down an interpersonal trigger for drinking—someone in your social network who is a heavy drinker or alcoholic (refer to your completed High-Risk Hierarchy and Your Social Network worksheet) and build your plan for dealing with this trigger. We have provided a sample plan for you to use as a model when designing your own (see Figure 3.4). For homework, you will complete two more self-management plans to deal with more heavy drinkers in your social network. Next week we will expand our use of self-management planning skills to other types of triggers—environmental, etc.

Self-Management Planning Sheet			
Trigger	**Plan**	**+/− Consequences**	**Difficulty (1–10)**
Husband invites heavy drinking neighbors over for impromptu barbecue at our house; they are drinking frozen daiquiris and beer. In fact, my husband asks me to keep the daiquiris coming while he tends the grill.	a. Abandon efforts to stay sober and join them.	a. + Have fun, fit in + Not embarrassed that not drinking + No need to deal with cravings − Let self down − Cravings intensify next week, harder to stay sober − Later resentful of husband − Lose control, drink too much	a. 4
	b. Leave home until the party is over.	b. + Avoid trigger + Avoid drinking − No one sober is watching the kids at home − Husband annoyed, neighbors baffled − Resentful of husband	b. 8
	c. Make myself frozen virgin coladas and stay busy at the grill and in the kitchen.	c. + Socialize + Enjoy a non alcoholic drink + Husband not annoyed − Still a high-risk situation, high cravings − Resentment toward husband	c. 5
	d. Approach husband the following week and discuss this and similar situations with him.	d. + Express feelings, be assertive + Possibly avoid future similar situations + Plan ahead − Husband may not wish to talk about it − May be frustrating	d. 10
	e. Remain pleasant to neighbors but don't join the barbecue—stay inside. Tell my husband I won't be able to make the daiquiris.	e. + Avoid trigger + Protecting right to self-care − Bored, resentful of husband − Neighbors think I'm rude	e. 10

Figure 3.4

Example of Completed Self-Management Planning Sheet for Heavy Drinkers in Social Network

Self-Management Planning Sheet

Trigger	Plan	+/− Consequences	Difficulty (1–10)
1.			
2.			

High-Risk Situations for the Week

Work with your therapist to identify at least one high-risk situation coming up in the next week. Write down ideas about how to handle this situation on the High-Risk Situations worksheet. Use the back of your self-recording card to record how you actually handled the anticipated situation, and write down any unexpected high-risk situations that may have arisen during the week.

High-Risk Situations

What high-risk situations do you think you may experience this week?

Situation 1:
How can you handle this situation?

a. _____

b. _____

c. _____

d. _____

Situation 2:
How can you handle this situation?

a. _____

b. _____

c. _____

d. _____

Situation 3:
How can you handle this situation?

a. _____

b. _____

c. _____

d. _____

Situation 4:
How can you handle this situation?

a. _____

b. _____

c. _____

d. _____

Homework

✎ Continue self-recording. Remember to use the back of your self-recording cards to write down the ways you handled your high-risk situations for the week.

✎ If not completed in session, finish creating your hierarchy of high-risk situations.

✎ Finish Your Social Network worksheet started in session.

✎ Finish Dealing With Heavy Drinkers in Your Social Network worksheet started in session.

✎ Complete a self-management plan for two of your drinking triggers related to heavy drinkers in your social network. A blank copy of the Self-Management Planning Sheet is provided at the end of the chapter.

✎ Choose two times during the week when you had a "strong urge" to drink and develop a behavior chain for each. A blank Behavior Chain worksheet is provided at the end of the chapter.

✎ Review the information in this chapter.

Self-Management Planning Sheet

Trigger	Plan	+/− Consequences	Difficulty (1–10)
I.			
2.			

Behavior Chain

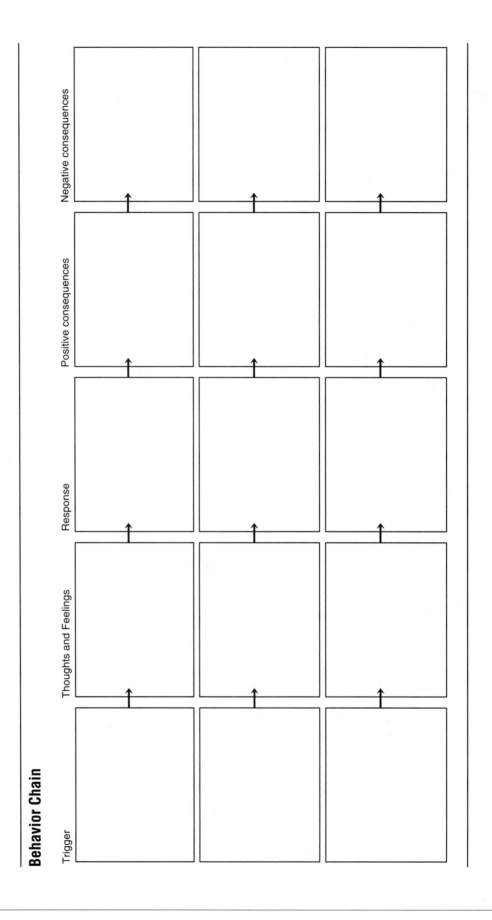

Trigger

Thoughts and Feelings

Response

Positive consequences

Negative consequences

Chapter 4

Session 4: *Enhancing Motivation to Change*

Goals

- To work out a self-management plan for triggers from your High-Risk Hierarchy

- To think about your reasons for wanting to quit drinking

- To start using negative consequences cards

Graphing Progress

In session, you will review the week with your therapist and together update your Alcohol Use and Urges Graph in Chapter 2 using the information from your most recently completed self-recording cards.

Self-Management Planning

Last session focused on self-management planning for triggers related to heavy drinkers in your social network. This session focuses on self-management planning for other triggers. See Figure 4.1 for an example of a Self-Management Planning Sheet. Choose triggers from your High-Risk Hierarchy, and work out a self-management plan for that trigger using the Self-Management Planning Sheet provided.

Self-Management Planning Sheet

Trigger	Plan	+/− Consequences	Difficulty (1–10)
Going to a restaurant for lunch	1. Don't eat lunch	+ Avoid trigger − Will be hungry	9
	2. Eat lunch at work	+ Avoid trigger + Won't be hungry + Will save money − Boring	5
	3. Go to a restaurant that doesn't serve liquor	+ Avoid trigger − Coworkers may not agree − Loss of privacy	3
	4. Learn to refuse when coworkers urge you to order a drink	+ Don't need to switch restaurants − May feel uncomfortable − Loss of privacy − Still faced with difficult trigger	8
Keeping liquor in the house	1. Never buy liquor	+ Save money + Avoid trigger − Partner can't drink at home − Company can't drink	5
	2. Hide the liquor	+ Avoid trigger − Inconvenient − I can find it	9
	3. Don't invite people over who drink	+ Avoid trigger − Lose friends	8
	4. Don't serve liquor to guests	+ Save money + Put myself first − Some people may be offended	7
	5. Buy liquor right before guests arrive and throw out the extra after they leave	+ Avoid offending guests + Minimize exposure to trigger − May waste money	2

Figure 4.1

Example of Completed Self-Management Planning Sheet

Self-Management Planning Sheet

Trigger	Plan	+/− Consequences	Difficulty (1–10)
I.			
2.			

Even though you have entered treatment, you probably have some mixed feelings about being in therapy and about actually making major changes in your life. This is a common feeling. You don't know what things will be like in the future, and that makes it somewhat frightening. In contrast, you do know what things are like now. Sometimes the familiar is comforting, even if it is unhappy. You are also giving up something that has provided good things in your life. Most people get pleasure from drinking—they enjoy the taste, like the sensations, and associate it with many good things in their lives. Giving it up is like saying good-bye to a friend you will miss, even though you know that alcohol is not a friend that has your best interests in mind. Having mixed feelings about giving up alcohol is perfectly natural.

You may also have mixed feelings about abstinence. Some people feel that it's impossible to have fun without alcohol or feel that it's the only way they can relax.

Review the section that follows and think about some of the pros and cons of drinking and not drinking. In thinking about the pros and cons, it may be helpful to think about short-term consequences and long-term consequences.

The Good, the Bad, and the Ugly of Drinking

STOP! Why do you want to quit drinking?

Before moving on, look at the good and bad things about your drinking. You probably have mixed feelings about stopping your drinking. It will help to stay motivated if you know why you wish to quit.

Think about the things that happen when you drink. These things are called consequences. Some consequences are good and others are bad. Most of the time, the good consequences happen right when you are drinking, and the bad consequences come later.

There are reasons why you drink. These come from the good things that happen, even if the good things only happen sometimes. Your mind and body remember these things.

The bad consequences can come right when you are drinking (like getting sick or having a fight) or can come later (like not being able to get up the next morning or having your children upset with you).

It will be easier to quit if you have a list of the bad things about drinking. The more you remember the bad things, the easier it is to say no when you have an urge to drink.

Also think about what's good and bad about quitting drinking. Some people don't think ahead when they make a change in their life. You will be more successful if you look ahead to see the good and bad things about making a change. Thinking about what you lose and what you get makes it easier to stay motivated.

Take a moment and start writing down the things that happen to you when you drink. Write down the things that happen right away and the things that happen later. Examples of consequences are:

- Physical effects: body sensations, getting sick, headaches, etc.

- Negative feelings

- Depressing thoughts

- Things that happen with other people, such as family or friends

- Money or legal trouble

- Work problems

See Figure 4.2 for an example of a completed decisional matrix. On the blank Decisional Matrix sheet provided, write down the good and bad things that happen right away (immediate consequences) when you drink. Also write down the good and bad things that happen later (delayed consequences) after drinking. Write these in the section marked "Continued Alcohol Use."

Do the same thing for quitting drinking. Write down the good and bad things that will happen right away when you stop drinking. Then write down the good and bad things that will come to you later. Write these in the section marked "Abstinence."

Remember to be realistic! It is important to be honest. The more you understand the reasons why you drink, the easier it will be to find a solution. When you are done, you should have more good reasons for stopping drinking than for keeping things the way they are.

Decisional Matrix

Abstinence

Pros (short- and long-term)	Cons (short- and long-term)
Stay alive	Hard to be in my skin
Get along with my partner better	Will miss drinking
My children will respect me more	May experience withdrawal symptoms
I will respect myself	Have to face negative emotions without alcohol
Save money	

Continued alcohol use

Pros (short- and long-term)	Cons (short- and long-term)
Makes me feel better, bad feelings go away	I could lose my job
Good way to get even with my partner when we're fighting	I could lose visitation with my children
Allows me to let loose and have a good time	I could become physically violent
Don't need to fight cravings	I will probably fight with my partner more
	I may experience blackouts
	I could end up in the hospital

Figure 4.2

Example of Completed Decisional Matrix

Decisional Matrix

Abstinence

Pros (short- and long-term)

_____

_____

_____

_____

_____

_____

_____

_____

Cons (short- and long-term)

_____

_____

_____

_____

_____

_____

_____

_____

Continued alcohol use

Pros (short- and long-term)

_____

_____

_____

_____

_____

_____

_____

_____

Cons (short- and long-term)

_____

_____

_____

_____

_____

_____

_____

_____

Use of Negative Consequences Cards

Before you take a drink, it is likely that you think about the short-term positive consequences of drinking. What you should begin doing is **thinking** about the negative consequences of drinking before you drink. The following exercise will help you start getting used to thinking about the cons of drinking, rather than the pros. This is one way of controlling your thoughts to help you avoid drinking.

Review your Decisional Matrix and the negative consequences of drinking that you listed. Write these consequences on a 3×5 index card and display it somewhere that you will see it often.

High-Risk Situations for the Week

Work with your therapist to identify at least one high-risk situation coming up in the next week. Write down ideas about how to handle this situation on the High-Risk Situations worksheet. Use the back of your self-recording card to record how you actually handled the anticipated situation, and write down any unexpected high-risk situations that may have arisen during the week.

High-Risk Situations

What high-risk situations do you think you may experience this week?

Situation 1:
How can you handle this situation?

a. _____

b. _____

c. _____

d. _____

Situation 2:
How can you handle this situation?

a. _____

b. _____

c. _____

d. _____

Situation 3:
How can you handle this situation?

a. _____

b. _____

c. _____

d. _____

Situation 4:
How can you handle this situation?

a. _____

b. _____

c. _____

d. _____

Homewk

✎ Continue self-recording. Remember to use the back of your self-recording cards to write down the ways you handled your high-risk situations for the week.

✎ Complete self-management plans for triggers not yet addressed. Blank copies of the Self-Management Planning Sheet are provided at the end of the chapter.

✎ If not completed in session, finish filling out the Decisional Matrix.

✎ Implement self-management plans and write on the back of your self-recording cards how you dealt with the triggers.

✎ Review the information in this chapter.

Self-Management Planning Sheet

Trigger	Plan	+/− Consequences	Difficulty (1–10)
1.			
2.			

Self-Management Planning Sheet

Trigger	Plan	+/− Consequences	Difficulty (1–10)
1.			
2.			

Chapter 5

Session 5: Assessing Anxiety and Depression / Dealing With Urges

Goals

- To assess any anxiety or depression you may be experiencing

- To learn ways of coping with your urges to drink

- To review the skills you have learned and the progress you have made up to this point

Graphing Progress

In session, you will review the week with your therapist and together update your Alcohol Use and Urge Graph in Chapter 2 using the information from your most recently completed self-recording cards.

Taking Stock of Anxiety

(Adapted in part from *How to Control Your Anxiety before it Controls You*, by Albert Ellis)

These are some common anxiety symptoms. Put a checkmark next to the ones you have experienced.

Breathing/Chest Symptoms
Shortness of breath
Rapid or shallow breathing
Pressure on chest
Lump in throat
Choking sensations

Skin-Related Symptoms
Sweating
Hot and cold spells
Itching

Heart/Blood Pressure Symptoms
Heart Racing
Palpitations
Faintness
Increased/decreased blood pressure

Intestinal Symptoms
Loss of appetite
Nausea or vomiting
Stomach discomfort

Muscular Symptoms
Shaking, tremors
Eyelid twitching
Startle reactions
Pacing
Insomnia
Fidgeting
Insomnia

Cognitive/Emotional Symptoms
Intrusive thoughts
Nightmares
Depersonalization (feeling outside of yourself)
Brief hallucinations
Paranoia and fear
Obsessing with no relief
Consistent worry about everyday events

Behavioral Symptoms
Avoidance
Irritability
Compulsive, repetitive acts

Which have you experienced and when?

_____

_____

_____

_____

What have you done to try to get relief?

_____

_____

_____

_____

Complete the What Do You Get Anxious About? worksheet to help you identify what types of things make you anxious, how you feel when you are anxious, and what works to make you less anxious.

What Do You Get Anxious About?

Social Anxiety:
Socializing
Public speaking
Job-related things
Being the center of attention

Post-Traumatic Stress:
Memories of traumatic events

Generalized Anxiety:
Thinking about things that could go wrong
Thoughts about not being able to pay the bills
Thoughts about people I love getting hurt

Panic Attacks:
Being nervous about having a panic attack
Fear of dying from a panic attack

Specific Phobias:
Open places
Closed places
Heights
Trains, planes
Cars, bridges, tunnels
Animals

Obsessions/Compulsions:
Intrusive thoughts
Feeling very detached
Fear of germs
Fear of hurting others
Fear of being bad
Checking for safety

What types of things do I get anxious about? _____

_____

_____

_____

_____

How do I feel when I'm anxious? _____

_____

_____

_____

What works to make me less anxious? _____

_____

_____

_____

Log of Anxiety Situations and Thoughts

Keep a log this week of situations or thoughts that make you feel anxious. Rate each one from 0 to 10.

Date	Time	Situation	Thought	Anxiety level 0–10
8/2/08	5 a.m.	Wake up, laying in bed	Why can't I sleep? What if I never get a full night's sleep again?	7
8/2/08	5 a.m.	Same	I'm so tired. What if I nod off at work?	6
8/2/08	5 a.m.	Same	What if they say I need to work late tonight? I'll never wake up in time for my trip tomorrow.	7
8/3/08	6 a.m.	Wake up, lay in bed	Up again. What if I'm so anxious on the plane that I freak out?	7
8/4/08	4 p.m.	Getting ready to go out for dinner	What if I'm so nervous at dinner I freeze and lose my train of thought? What if they all think I'm a loser? I'll look so stupid and nerdy.	9
8/6/08	8 a.m.	Driving to work	I acted like such an idiot yesterday—they will all know I don't know what I'm talking about. What if I lose my job over this?	8

Figure 5.1

Example of Completed Log of Anxiety Situations and Thoughts

If anxiety is a problem for you, your therapist may ask you to keep a daily log of anxiety triggers and thoughts (see Figure 5.1). You can photocopy the Log of Anxiety Situations and Thoughts worksheet as needed. Write down your actual thoughts; these often start with "I." Next week you will review the log with your therapist and discuss ways to cope with anxiety.

Log of Anxiety Situations and Thoughts

Keep a log this week of situations or thoughts that make you feel anxious. Rate each one from 0 to 10.

Date	Time	Situation	Thought	Anxiety level 0–10
____	____	_____	_____	____
____	____	_____	_____	____
____	____	_____	_____	____
____	____	_____	_____	____
____	____	_____	_____	____
____	____	_____	_____	____
____	____	_____	_____	____
____	____	_____	_____	____
____	____	_____	_____	____
____	____	_____	_____	____
____	____	_____	_____	____
____	____	_____	_____	____
____	____	_____	_____	____
____	____	_____	_____	____
____	____	_____	_____	____
____	____	_____	_____	____

We all feel sad from time to time. Passing feelings of sadness or depression are normal and common. Like anxiety, feelings of sadness and depression can be triggers to drink excessively, and, like anxiety, depression is usually made worse in the long run by excessive drinking. So, it's important for you to keep aware of your moods and to be able to change your moods through methods that do not involve alcohol.

Complete the worksheet titled "What Do You Get Depressed About?" to identify symptoms of depression you may have been experiencing recently. You and your therapist will also discuss types of situations that have made you feel depressed in the past in order to figure out how you can cope with these situations without drinking.

What Do You Get Depressed About?

These are some common symptoms of depression:

- Depressed mood
- Sadness
- Apathy
- Tearful
- Feeling empty
- Thoughts of death, thoughts of suicide
- Decreased interest in things you used to enjoy
- Sleeping more than usual or unable to sleep

- Feeling worthless, low self-esteem
- Fatigue or loss of energy
- Feelings of hopelessness
- Waking up at 4 or 5 a.m.
- Difficulty concentrating
- Change in appetite
- Moving slowly

What situations tend to make you feel depressed? _____

_____

_____

What thoughts tend to make you feel depressed? _____

_____

_____

How do you feel when you are depressed? _____

_____

_____

What works to make you feel less depressed? _____

_____

_____

_____

Remember that drinking may be a short-term solution to escape feelings of sadness and depression, but in the long run, it makes the depression worse and also creates a new set of problems that themselves can cause depression. With the help of your therapist, you will find a way out of the vicious cycle.

If you have been struggling with depression, fill in the Log of Depressing Situations and Thoughts during the week (see Figure 5.2). A blank copy is provided in this chapter for photocopying. Next session you will review the log with your therapist and discuss ways to cope with depression.

Log of Depressing Situations and Thoughts

Keep a log this week of situations or thoughts that make you feel sad or depressed. Rate each one from 0 to 10. We'll go over it next week.

Date	Time	Situation	Thought	Depression level 0–10
9/6/08	4 a.m.	Can't sleep, lay in bed	Oh my. I feel awful. So depressed. I don't want to go to work today. I can't sleep what's wrong with me?	9
9/6/08	5:30 a.m.	Get out of bed	Oh man—what's the point of showering. Too tired. Will call in sick. Can't face work today. Work is stupid and I don't contribute anyway.	9
9/6/08	7 a.m.	Driving to work	Dragged myself through the morning routine. I feel awful. I will end up an old lady alone all the time, will die alone in a bare room. What's the point. My life is so not where it was supposed to be at this age.	7
9/7/08	6 a.m.	In shower	I'm so tired. Who cares about work. I can't take this feeling much longer. Ugh—have to choke down some breakfast or will get a headache. Ah—who cares, don't feel like eating. Who cares if I get a headache.	9
9/9/08	6 p.m.	Get home from work	Alone again. I've managed to alienate or isolate from everyone in my life who used to love me. Now no one calls or cares. Serves me right. What a loser.	7

Figure 5.2

Example of Completed Log of Depressing Situations and Thoughts

Log of Depressing Situations and Thoughts

Keep a log this week of situations or thoughts that make you feel sad or depressed. Rate each one from 0 to 10. We'll go over it next week.

Date	Time	Situation	Thought	Depression level 0–10

Alcohol depresses (slows down) your central nervous system, but it tricks you first!

In the short run, alcohol makes you feel euphoric, happy, and relaxed. In this way, it feels at first like a stimulant, but this is because it is suppressing ("depressing") the parts of your brain that make you feel inhibited or anxious.

When the alcohol increases in your system to a certain point, it can make you feel depressed, irritable, or angry.

When the alcohol leaves your system, *the withdrawal effects are opposite those of the initial effects of relaxation and happiness.* That is, you feel a "rebound effect" of anxiety—even more anxious!! You may also feel depressed, irritable, or restless.

In other words, the use of alcohol *temporarily* (and artificially) erases the negative feelings (anxiety, depression) that made you want to drink in the first place, but then actually *magnifies* (increases) the very same anxiety and depressive symptoms that made you want to drink. Now you feel even more anxious and depressed—which makes you feel like you need to drink again, to get rid of those feelings again.

It's a vicious cycle. When experiencing the increased anxiety/depression withdrawal symptoms after alcohol, it's common for people to think, "Wow, I must be really anxious (depressed)—even more than I thought. If I don't have alcohol in my system, I feel REALLY anxious. I'd better have a drink to calm my nerves again and get rid of this awful anxiety (prevent another panic attack, stop these obsessive thoughts)."

Many people don't realize that it's actually the *alcohol itself* that is causing an increase in the anxiety or depression!

Getting Off the Rollercoaster

The only way to stop this vicious cycle is to *get off the roller coaster*—to stop drinking and learn to cope with the anxiety and depression that led you to drink in the first place. Longer-term solutions take time to learn and practice. *You have to tolerate a certain amount of discomfort while you are learning to control your anxiety and depression without alcohol.*

There are nonaddictive antidepressant medications available to help as well. You may want to discuss this with an American Society of Addictions Medicine (ASAM) physician or a psychiatrist with additional accreditation from the American Academy of Addiction Psychiatry—these physicians are best equipped to treat alcohol-dependent patients for psychiatric problems.

Coping With Desires to Drink

This week, your therapist will offer you some ways to handle urges to drink.

Most people have urges to drink when they first quit. In the beginning, these urges happen often and can get very intense. The good news: After a while, the urges get easier to ignore.

Here are some things to remember about urges and triggers:

- Urges are reactions to triggers. Your body has learned to connect certain people, places, and things to drinking. The triggers can even be thoughts or emotions.

- Urges are a sign that you have to do something different. Something in the situation is making it difficult for you. The way you handle the situation has to change.

- Urges to drink don't last forever! They are like waves in the ocean—they peak, they crest, and they subside. They usually go away in a short time. Even though the few minutes can seem very long, remember that the desire to drink will go away if you give it time.

Here are some ways to deal with an urge. Pick one or more that will work for you:

- Remind yourself that the urge is a temporary thing. No matter how bad it is, it will not last forever.

- If possible, get away from the situation that created the trigger.

- Go through the list of reasons why you decided to stop drinking. Remind yourself about the bad parts of drinking. Remind yourself about the good things about not drinking.

- Find something to do that will get your mind off the urge to drink. A fun activity that does not involve drinking will help distract you from the struggle.

- Talk with someone who will be understanding and supportive. Often just talking about the urge will take some pressure off you.

- Say encouraging things to yourself that make you feel good about not drinking.

- Use your imagination. Imagine yourself in a pleasant place where you are peaceful and happy.

- Another way to use your imagination is to have a picture in your head of the urge looking like an ugly monster. Think of yourself as a ninja or a samurai fighting back and beating the monster. Or picture bleach poured in a wineglass.

- Imagine that you are in a boat and the urge is a big wave that comes and rocks the boat, but then passes you by.

- Tell yourself you can't always control when an urge comes, but you can just accept that "there's that urge again," and let it stay until it evaporates. Don't try to get rid of it, just notice it, distract yourself, and let it go away when it's ready.

- Pray.

- Read through your workbook and do exercises you find helpful, such as a behavior chain for that particular urge.

- Journal.

- Talk to a qualified physician (preferably accredited by the American Academy of Addiction Psychiatry or an ASAM-Certified Physician) about the option of medication to help reduce cravings for alcohol. Research has supported the usefulness of these medicines: naltrexone (ReVia®) and acamprosate (Campral®). Other medications are currently in various stages of research and development.

These are some techniques used by people to fight off the urges. We give you a list because we know that everyone is different. However, we know that people have used these techniques to be successful.

Remember, urges get weaker over time. You will gain more confidence and pride in your ability to beat them.

Write down some ideas for dealing with your urges in the space provided.

Dealing With Urges
In response to an urge or craving to drink, I can . . .

_____

_____

_____

_____

_____

_____

_____

Look How Far You've Come

Review the following information with your therapist to highlight your progress over the past few weeks, as well as the new skills you've learned. This section also lists the topics you have yet to cover as part of the treatment program. This is to give you the "big picture" of the treatment plan and to help you see how much progress you've made here and how many new skills you now have under your belt.

You have already learned a great deal in treatment. You have been practicing many skills to help keep you from drinking. You understand alcohol better, in terms of standard drinks, blood alcohol level, and problem levels of drinking. You have been doing self-recording, learning to recognize your triggers, and gaining insight into the behavior chain that leads to drinking after you encounter one of your triggers.

You've learned what cues in the world around you may start you feeling and thinking your way toward drinking. You've figured out which risky situations are going to be the toughest for you—and since forewarned is forearmed, now you can be prepared. And you have learned to see well ahead of time that these situations are coming up, so now you can plan accordingly. You'll see the trouble before you are right on top of it! You've analyzed your social network and identified people who may be triggers for drinking as well as nondrinkers who may be potential buffers for you against drinking. You've learned to generate plans for dealing with triggers, so that you are prepared with a specific way to deal with each one.

You have considered the pros and cons of drinking and of abstinence, so that you may feel more strongly that the pros of abstinence outweigh the pros of drinking. You are also clearer on the cons of drinking.

You have some new tools to deal with urges and cravings.

You have learned to identify types of negative emotions and symptoms.

You're on your way! Stay tuned . . . you'll be learning to:

- Calm yourself when anxious or sad

- Speak assertively

- Create more rewards for sobriety to replace the positive consequences of drinking

- Recognize the negative consequences of drinking

- Challenge thoughts about alcohol that get you into trouble

- Deal effectively with situations where alcohol is present

- Make less risky decisions

- Solve problems effectively

- Manage angry thoughts, feelings, and behavior better

- Identify warning signs that could lead to relapses

- Avoid relapses and deal with any slips

High-Risk Situations for the Week

Work with your therapist to identify at least one high-risk situation coming up in the next week. Write down ideas about how to handle this situation on the High-Risk Situations worksheet. Use the back of your self-recording card to record how you actually handled the anticipated situation, and write down any unexpected high-risk situations that may have arisen during the week.

High-Risk Situations

What high-risk situations do you think you may experience this week?

Situation 1:
How can you handle this situation?

a. _____

b. _____

c. _____

d. _____

Situation 2:
How can you handle this situation?

a. _____

b. _____

c. _____

d. _____

Situation 3:
How can you handle this situation?

a. _____

b. _____

c. _____

d. _____

Situation 4:
How can you handle this situation?

a. _____

b. _____

c. _____

d. _____

Homework

✎ Continue self-recording. Remember to use the back of your self-recording cards to write down the ways you handled your high-risk situations for the week.

✎ Finish What Do You Get Anxious About? worksheet started in session.

✎ If relevant, keep a Log of Anxiety Situations and Thoughts.

✎ Finish What Do You Get Depressed About? worksheet started in session.

✎ If relevant, keep a Log of Depressing Situations and Thoughts.

✎ Complete two more self-management plans for more difficult items on your High-Risk Hierarchy. A blank copy of the Self-Management Planning Sheet is provided at the end of the chapter.

✎ Use urge coping twice during the week in a high-risk situation or another time when experiencing an urge.

✎ Review the information in this chapter.

Self-Management Planning Sheet

Trigger	Plan	+/− Consequences	Difficulty (1–10)
I.			
2.			

Chapter 6

Session 6: Affect and Mood Management / Rearranging Behavioral Consequences

Goals

- To learn how to cope with anxiety and depression

- To challenge negative thoughts

- To practice relaxation

- To learn how to let things go

- To discover alternative activities that you can engage in instead of drinking

- To learn ways of increasing the positive rewards of staying sober

Graphing Progress

In session, you will review the week with your therapist and together update your Alcohol Use and Urges Graph in Chapter 2 using the information from your most recently completed self-recording cards.

Challenging Negative Thoughts

Negative events can be thought of as emotion triggers. They lead to negative thoughts, which then lead to negative feelings and behavior. If you can learn to identify, challenge, and replace negative thoughts, you can avoid or alleviate anxious and depressed feelings and related behaviors. See the following example.

Example of Challenging Negative Thoughts

Jane has been sober for 2 months now, thanks to hard work on her part. She is feeling particularly proud of herself this weekend. She managed to attend a wedding on Saturday and didn't have a slip even though there was an open bar. On Sunday morning, she is thinking that maybe she and her boyfriend, with his two kids, will take a ride to the beach. But when he wakes up, he says that he forgot to tell her that he promised his kids that he would take them on a fishing boat that day. He tells her that she's welcome to come with them if she wants. Jane feels herself getting upset. She thinks, "I get nauseous on those boats so I don't want to go. Now I'll be stuck here all day alone, with nothing to do. My life is empty. I don't have my own kids. I probably would have been a bad mother anyway. I'm such a loser, of course John doesn't want to spend the day with me." In past similar situations, she might have stayed quiet, cried when they left, and then stayed home watching TV and feeling sad. Today, instead she challenged and replaced her negative thoughts:

Negative Thought: (emotion generated: *sadness*)

Now I'll be stuck here all day alone, with nothing to do. My life is empty.

Challenge and Replace (emotions generated: *relief, excitement*):

Wait a minute—I'm not stuck. I can still go to the beach—I'll create my own fun day.

Negative Thought: (emotion generated: *sadness*)

I don't have my own kids. I probably would have been a bad mother anyway.

Challenge and Replace (emotions generated: *relief, contentment*):

I didn't want to have children with my first husband, and that was an excellent decision. I love John and I love his kids, so we decided not to have kids of our own. I've been happy with that decision too. It's just at times like this that I regret my decisions, but I know they were the right decisions for me at the time. And John's kids and I have a nice relationship.

Negative Thought: (emotion generated: *depression*)

I'm such a loser. Of course John doesn't want to spend the day with me.

Challenge and Replace (emotions generated: *confidence, positive anticipation*)

Loser schmoozer. John asked me to go with them, silly!! It's a beautiful day out and I'm not going to waste my time feeling sorry for myself. I'll call my girlfriend and see if she wants to spend the day at the beach. Maybe I'll make us a banana bread to snack on . . .

Types of Negative Thoughts

Negative emotion thoughts can be classified into types. It is easier to challenge and replace a negative thought after identifying and figuring out which type of negative thought it is. See the list on the following pages for the different types of negative emotion thoughts. Which ones ring a bell for you? If completed for homework, classify the thoughts in your logs of anxious and depressing thoughts.

All or Nothing Thinking: This type of thinking ignores the possibility that some things are between all good and all bad. Example: *"I must always do a perfect job."*

Overgeneralization: Overgeneralization happens when people see one bad experience as evidence of everything being bad. Example: *"I lost that account; I am a crummy account executive."*

Mental Filter: A negative mental filter keeps out positive thoughts and focuses on negative things. People who always see "the glass as half empty" have a negative mental filter. Example: *"I am extremely unattractive—just look at that fly-away hair."*

Disqualifying the Positive: This problem thinking happens when a person believes that good things that happen are unusual or somehow do not count. Example: *"I got a good grade on that test because it was so easy. Anyone could have gotten an A."*

Jumping to Conclusions: People often jump to conclusions without having evidence to support their negative interpretations. For instance, **Mind Reading** is jumping to the conclusion that you know what the other person is thinking. Example: *"My husband looked at me funny. He hates this new outfit I bought and is mad that I spent money on it."*

Catastrophizing: Catastrophizing happens when a person exaggerates the importance of things. A key to this type of thinking is someone thinking about how something is **awful**, **terrible**, or **horrible**. Example: *"Here I am, stuck in traffic.*

This is the third time this year I'll be late to the meeting. My boss is probably ready to fire me. I can't believe I let myself be late again."

Depression Filter. When people are depressed, they typically have thoughts that are quite negative, but this is because depression tends to distort the thinking process to result in an onslaught of negative self-talk. Example: *"I am really not where I should be at this stage of my life. At this rate, I have very little hope for improving my future."*

Should Statements: Some people set such high standards for themselves that they set themselves up for failure if they do not meet their standards of perfection. The key to catching this kind of thinking is the word *should*. Example: *"I should cook a full meal with a protein and vegetable every night and the whole family should sit down and eat it together, because I'm a good mother and that's what good mothers do."*

What If. This is a special type of anxiety thought that relates to worrying:

People worry about inability to do common everyday things:
> *"What if I run out of money this month and can't pay my rent?"*

Or they worry about being or going crazy:
> *"What if I'm really nuts and I end up in a mental hospital?"*

Or they worry about rare events:
> *"What if my doctor tells me I have cancer?"*

Or about having anxiety
> *"What if I have another panic attack while I'm driving the car?"*

[Adapted in part from David Burns (1980). *Feeling good: the new mood therapy.* New York: New American Library.]

Practice Challenging Negative Thoughts

You can practice identifying, challenging, and replacing negative thoughts, as well as identify which type of thought each of the negative thoughts is, using the Challenging Negative Thoughts worksheet. You may photocopy this form as needed.

Remember! Your thoughts are not facts! You can choose to go with negative thoughts or to leave them behind!

Challenging Negative Thoughts

Think about a situation where you felt depressed or anxious.

_____

_____

_____

Now list the **negative thoughts** you had, along with the emotion that went with that thought. Next, write a thought(s) that challenges and replaces each negative thought.

Negative thought (emotion generated: _____)

_____

_____

Challenge and replace thought (emotion generated: _____)

_____

_____

Negative thought (emotion generated: _____)

_____

_____

Challenge and replace thought (emotion generated: _____)

_____

_____

Negative thought (emotion generated: _____)

_____

_____

Challenge and replace thought (emotion generated: _____)

_____

_____

Tips to Manage Strong Negative Emotions

1. **Retain your calm and cool.** One of the destructive effects of strong emotion is mental confusion and its effect on judgment. As long as you can retain your cool, you will be in control of the situation. Here are some phrases you can say to yourself to help you cool off in a crisis:

   - *Time out.*
   - *I can handle this.*
   - *Take it easy.*
   - *Take a few deep breaths.*
   - *Hold it—don't do or say anything I'll regret later.*
   - *Easy does it.*
   - *Chill out.*
   - *Relax.*
   - *Count to ten.*
   - *Cool it.*

2. **Take a "time-out."** If you cannot immediately calm down use the "time-out" procedure to allow yourself time to get back in control of your anger and avoid "acting-out" your emotions and repeating past destructive behaviors. (See "Time-Out" handout for Session 9.)

3. **Slow down** and assess the situation. Identify and challenge negative thoughts.

4. **Stop catastrophizing.** Take a deep breath from the bottom of your stomach, and tell yourself you'll be fine. Remember, you are a good coper—you can cope with whatever comes your way, you just have to slow down and figure out the best way to proceed. Acting emotional will only make matters worse.

5. **Figure out what you can control** in this situation, and what is out of your control. Let go of what you can't control.

   You may find that you cannot resolve the situation and you still feel sad. Remember that you can't fix everything. Let yourself feel sad—it's a natural feeling and will go away after a while. Don't punish yourself for feeling sad.

6. **Congratulate yourself** for handling a difficult situation in a nonreactive way. You behaved in a self-respectful way, and did not let others or your own emotion get the better of you. You have also prevented yourself from spiraling downward into deeper anxiety or depression.

7. **Have we forgotten anything?**

   _____

   _____

   _____

To summarize and to manage strong emotions here are three ways to cope with anxiety and depression—(1) learning how to relax, (2) challenging and replacing negative thoughts, and (3) learning to let things go. See Tips to Manage Strong Negative Emotions for more strategies.

The goal is to recognize when you're starting to become anxious or depressed, so that you can stop yourself from spiraling downward into uncontrolled anxiety or sadness. You have more control over whether you feel sad or anxious in response to a situation than you think!

Similar to triggers to alcohol, there are triggers for anxiety and sadness. It's not always possible or desirable to avoid triggers for strong emotions, but you can learn how to change your thoughts and responses to such triggers.

Learning How to Relax

Most people experience anxiety or tension in their everyday lives: real problems occur, we worry about problems that might happen, and we worry about ourselves. All these worries create tension and anxiety.

Some people use alcohol to cope with feelings of tension, anxiety, or sadness. Alcohol may provide temporary relief, but the problems and worries don't go away. In fact, alcohol creates its own sets of problems and usually makes the anxiety and sadness worse in the long run. Instead of drinking, learning how to relax can help.

Having a few simple, quick ways to relax such as the following can come in handy when you start to feel anxious or depressed.

- Exercise

- Take a hot bath

- Get a massage

- Take a long walk or swim

- Use relaxation breathing to help to relieve tension—it's quick and simple to learn

An easy type of relaxation breathing is to take a deep breath from the abdomen (hold your hand on your stomach to make sure it's moving up and down with the breath) every 4–10 seconds. Inhale to a slow count of 6, and exhale to a slow count of 4. Do this for 5–10 min before or during an anxious situation to regulate your breathing and reduce anxiety, and/or every day for 20 min to have more long-lasting effects.

Remember, you can use relaxation breathing anywhere—all anyone might notice is how calm you are!

Identifying, Classifying, and Challenging Negative Thoughts

Use the skills you learned for identifying, classifying, challenging, and replacing negative affect thoughts. (See section "Types of Negative Emotion Thoughts" for types of thoughts.)

Letting Things Go

You can't control whether or not you'll have anxiety or depression thoughts. But you can control whether you let yourself get caught up in them, worry about them, obsess about them, and get even more anxious or depressed. Anxious and depressed thoughts are like a snowball rolling down a hill. They pick up speed, size, and strength as they go, if you let yourself get caught up. Let the negative thought float in one ear, recognize it, identify it, and classify it, and then let it float out the other ear. It can't hurt you. You are safe. You're fine. For instance:

Anxious Thought ("what if" thought):

"What if I lose my job and I can't pay my bills?"

To let go of that "what if" thought, observe that you've had that thought and that it made you feel anxious, then try thinking something like this next:

"There's that 'what if' thought again. I don't have time or energy to worry about that now—it would be a waste of time. Let it go when it's ready. Now where's that CD I like to listen to. . ."

Depressing Thought

"I've wasted so much time in my life drinking—I'll never get on track."

Again, notice that you've had this depressing thought and that it made you feel sad. Then try an alternative thought:

"I'm only 35 and I have plenty of time left, no sense wasting any more of it thinking depressing thoughts. I'm going to make the most of my time today. I think I'll go for a walk. Just because I had this thought doesn't make it true."

Rearranging Behavioral Consequences

This week you will learn ways to increase the positive rewards you experience from staying sober. You are also going to learn about other ways to increase the positive thoughts that you have about staying sober to and increase the negative thoughts that you have right now about drinking.

Refer back to your completed Decisional Matrix sheet from Chapter 4, and review the reasons you want to quit drinking and the consequences associated with drinking. Since it has been 2 weeks since you've completed the matrix, it makes sense to review it now and make any necessary changes or additions. You will discuss with your therapist the following two ways that you can use your matrix to help you become or stay sober.

Thinking Through the Drink

You have already been practicing thinking about the negative consequences of drinking several times a day when you read your 3×5 negative consequences card. Now, I'd like to extend that to have you keep the card with you in your wallet and take it out to read before you drink. Be sure to use these cards when specific situations that may lead to drinking come up. For example, if some friends call and invite you to meet them at a club or bar, your first thoughts will probably be related to the positive consequences of going out and getting a drink. Instead of giving your friends an answer right away, delay accepting their offer and review your index card. Practice your new thinking habit. Then, call back and decline the invitation, using these suggestions:

■ Be firm but polite—make it clear that you mean what you say when you decline.

■ Suggest an alternative—Even though you aren't going to go to the club, say you'd like to see them and you wonder if they would like to come over for dinner on Sunday.

Replacing the Positive Consequences of Drinking Positive Rewards of Sobriety

Next, review the positive consequences of drinking that you listed on your Decisional Matrix sheet.

Despite the negative consequences of drinking, you have to remember that the positive consequences are what kept you drinking and giving up those positive aspects of drinking is difficult. When people develop a drinking problem, they experience the "funneling effect": many resources—time, money, energy, attention—are directed toward alcohol, including thinking about alcohol, getting alcohol, drinking, being drunk, and recovering from alcohol's effects.

When people leave drinking behind, they often experience a frightening emptiness in their lives—the time and energy that drinking took has to be filled with something rewarding, to keep you from going back to drinking. Try to think of it like this: One advantage of not drinking is that you have newfound freedom to use your time and resources in new ways, in whatever ways you choose. Let's make that a conscious choice. Let's think of ways to replace some of the positive consequences of drinking with rewarding activities that will be fun, positive, and healthy. To help you with that, review the following list of activities that many people enjoy (Table 6.1).

Alternatives to Drinking to Get Similar Positive Rewards

Although some of the positive consequences of drinking (e.g., euphoria, relaxation) are not easily replaced, it is important to remember that they are artificial and temporary, and usually followed by negative consequences.

Review the positive consequences of drinking that you listed on your Decisional Matrix sheet, and develop a list of positive, rewarding alternatives to drinking (e.g., relaxation, social activities, enjoying nature). Record alternatives on the worksheet provided. Be sure to select activities that fit with your long-term goals. For example, if one of your long-term goals is to get into better shape, you may wish to engage in physical activities like jogging or biking.

Table 6.1 What Do Other People Do?

Read a book	On a rainy day, clean the house while dancing to loud music	Play basketball or tennis with your kids at the park
Go to the gym and work out	Sort through old photos and start a scrapbook	Take a long walk on the boardwalk
Go out for a nice meal	Surf the Web	Go to a meeting and out for coffee after
Do volunteer work	Go "treasure hunting" at garage sales on the weekends	Go to a free lecture at the local community college
Go to a county fair	Work backstage or build sets for your local community theater group	Do yard work and enjoy the fresh air
Play cards or board games	Get a massage, manicure or pedicure, or all three!	Take your dog to the park or for a brisk walk around the neighborhood
Wander the mall to find bargains	Call an old friend who lives far away	Paint a room in your home
Begin a knitting or carpentry project	Go to a sporting event	Sign up for a cooking class or art course
Go to a concert or play	Go to a museum or art gallery	Visit the zoo or aquarium
Go on a picnic at a park or take your picnic to the beach on a summer day	Lounge by the pool, or swim indoors at the YMCA	Go on a camping trip
Take a bike ride	Order in and watch a DVD	Go horseback riding
Go to Home Depot and buy materials for a new do-it-yourself home repair project	Run errands	Play basketball at the park
Take a dance or martial arts class	Go into the city and window shop	Go to services at your house of worship
Plant a vegetable garden or flowers	Catch fireflies	Buy new fancy bodywash Take a shower or bath
Call or visit your grandchildren, or a favorite niece or nephew	Make a nice dinner	Plan a trip someplace new
Join a book club or go to the library or book store to find a great novel to read	Go rollerblading	Volunteer at your local place of worship

High-Risk Situations for the Week

Work with your therapist to identify at least one high-risk situation coming up in the next week. Write down ideas about how to handle this situation on the High-Risk Situations worksheet. Use the back of your self-recording card to record how you actually handled the anticipated situation, and write down any unexpected high-risk situations that may have arisen during the week.

Alternatives to Drinking

Trigger situation and positive consequences of alcohol	Alternative activity with similar positive consequence
Some examples:	
Saturday night at restaurant with spouse (positive consequences of alcohol: relaxation, wine goes with dinner, euphoria, festive atmosphere)	Get my favorite take-out food to eat at home and then go out to movie.
Tuesday night, spouse working late, and no one is home (positive consequences of alcohol: reduce loneliness, special time alone, relaxation)	Join a gym and go swimming Tuesday night, then stop on way home at Starbucks for decaf drink or browse the local bookstore.
Friday, after work, doing yard work (positive consequences of alcohol: relaxation)	Stop at gym to exercise on way home. Do the yard work Saturday morning instead.
Neighborhood picnic, Fourth of July (positive consequences of alcohol: more sociable, festive atmosphere, euphoria)	Go to gym before picnic, then bring my own soda. If too many tempting triggers at picnic, leave.

High-Risk Situations

What high-risk situations do you think you may experience this week?

Situation 1:
How can you handle this situation?

a. _____

b. _____

c. _____

d. _____

Situation 2:
How can you handle this situation?

a. _____

b. _____

c. _____

d. _____

Situation 3:
How can you handle this situation?

a. _____

b. _____

c. _____

d. _____

Situation 4:
How can you handle this situation?

a. _____

b. _____

c. _____

d. _____

Homework

✏ Continue self-recording. Remember to use the back of your self-recording cards to write down the ways you handled your high-risk situations for the week.

✏ Continue keeping a Log of Anxiety Thoughts and/or Log of Depressing Thoughts if useful for you.

✏ Finish worksheet Challenging Negative Thoughts. This week, try to catch yourself with anxious or sad thoughts, challenge them, and replace them.

✏ Use relaxation skills two times this week, and write down on back of self-recording card when you do.

✏ Continue implementation of self-management plans. A blank copy of the Self-Management Planning Sheet is provided at the end of the chapter.

✏ If not completed in session, finish filling out the Alternatives to Drinking worksheet and practice two alternatives this week.

✏ Hang negative consequences card where it is visible and read on a daily basis.

✏ Review the information in this chapter.

Self-Management Planning Sheet

Trigger	Plan	+/− Consequences	Difficulty (1–10)
1.			
2.			

Chapter 7

Session 7: Connecting With Others / Dealing With Alcohol-Related Thoughts

Goals

- To improve your social support for abstinence

- To learn to challenge and replace your dangerous thoughts about alcohol that lead to drinking

Graphing Progress

In session, you will review the week with your therapist and together update your Alcohol Use and Urges Graph in Chapter 2 using the information from your most recently completed self-recording cards.

Improving Social Support for Abstinence

Session 3 discussed how to manage heavy drinkers in your social support network as a way to help you become and stay abstinent. It's also very important to develop a stable personal support network of nondrinkers or other people who support your abstinence and whom you can enjoy, spend time with, turn to when you have troubles, and who need you. You have been learning to cope well, be autonomous, and know how to take care of yourself, that is, be your own best friend. In addition to this, a nice sober social support network will enrich your life, provide you with opportunities for growth, warmth, and happiness, and be there when you need a shoulder.

Remember, part of taking care of yourself is providing yourself with a richer, healthy network of connections and knowing when and how to reach out to people who want to help you—people who have your best interest in mind and who treat you well. You do not need to do this alone!

Social Support Network Exercise

Update Your Social Network worksheet from Session 3 (make changes, add any new members). How has your social network changed over the past weeks since you stopped drinking? Are you content with your current sober support network? Do you feel "connected" to the people in your social network?

Making Connections

What kind of people do you want to connect with? The following worksheet (I Want to Connect With People Who) can help you identify what you are looking for in members of your network. You may also find it helpful to write your thoughts and feelings about your social network in a journal.

You deserve to be around people who treat you well and to *not* be with people who treat you poorly or do not have your best interest in mind. This worksheet is *not* for the purpose of thinking about the characteristics of a "perfect mate," but rather is designed to help you think of how you want to be treated by people in your current or new social network. Some people are lucky enough to have great social networks "built in" to their families—supportive siblings, for example—or their neighborhoods—a circle of friendly neighbors, for instance. Others have to make more of an effort to develop a social network that they value. Remember, social networks can consist of different types of "friends"—romantic partners, children, relatives, friends, AA members, professional counselors, community-based networks, etc.

Use the Making Connections worksheet to brainstorm ways to find and develop your social network. In completing the worksheet, you can use any term you feel comfortable with–friend, significant other, social support person, etc. See Figure 7.1 for a completed example.

I Want to Connect With People Who

* I like and respect
* I have fun with
* I trust
* I feel safe with
* I care about
* I am in touch with or see often
* Care about me
* Don't put me down
* Respect my wishes
* Are not always needy themselves
* Know how to give and take
* Have time for me
* Understand about addiction
* I enjoy myself with

* _____
* _____
* _____
* _____
* _____

Journaling

Some people find it helpful to write down their thoughts and feelings in a journal. You can start with answers to these questions:

1. Do I have people in my life who I feel I can count on when I need it?

_____

2. Do I have people in my life who count on me?

_____

3. Do I believe that others can help me?

_____

4. How do I feel about other knowing that I have a problem and need them?

_____

Brainstorm by category ways for you to connect with others to establish a strong, healthy social network.

How can you . . .

- **Connect with friends?**

  (Volunteer organizations, classes, reconnecting with old friends)

  I will attend my high school reunion and reconnect with some people I miss.

  I will dig up the numbers of two women I used to be friendly with—they are only 30–40 minutes away.

  I will take a baking class at the local community college.

- **Connect with community-based networks?**

  (AA, professional counselors, clubs, religious affiliations, special interest groups)

  I will go to 4 AA meetings a week—women's meetings.

  I will volunteer at my church and start attending services.

  I will go on the Web to see if there are biking clubs in my town.

- **Connect with children and relatives as part of your social support network?**

  I will call my sisters each once per week to say hi.

  I start a vegetable garden and perennial plant garden project with my kid.

  I will visit my Mom and Dad at least once a month even though it's a 90 min ride.

- **Connect with a romantic partner as part of your social support network?**

  I will join a dating website to see what it's like.

  I will remind my friends that I am available if they know anyone for a blind date.

Figure 7.1

Example of Completed Making Connections Worksheet

Making Connections

Brainstorm by category ways for you to connect with others to establish a strong, healthy social network.

How can you . . .

◾ **Connect with friends?**
(Volunteer organizations, classes, reconnecting with old friends)

_____

_____

_____

◾ **Connect with community-based networks?**
(AA, professional counselors, clubs, religious affiliations, special interest groups)

_____

_____

_____

◾ **Connect with children and relatives as part of your social support network?**

_____

_____

_____

◾ **Connect with a romantic partner as part of your social support network?**

_____

_____

_____

In this week's session, you will work with your therapist to restructure your thoughts about alcohol so they no longer serve as triggers for drinking.

Your thoughts lead to actions. People often do not realize how powerful their thoughts are. Sometimes these thoughts happen so quickly that people believe they are acting without thinking. If you could have an instant replay in slow motion, you could see how your thoughts lead to your actions.

Three types of thoughts can lead to drinking (see also Figure 7.2):

1. Thoughts or images about alcohol can create urges. Some examples are images of bars, thoughts about your favorite drink, and smells and sounds of alcohol. These thoughts directly trigger urges.

2. Thoughts about the enjoyable effects of alcohol can trigger urges. Some examples are, "Just one won't hurt"; "It will calm my nerves"; "My friends will think I'm strange if I don't have a drink"; "It will help me sleep"; or "I can just have one." You probably have some of these thoughts listed as positive consequences on your Decisional Matrix from Session 4. These thoughts are generally about the short-term benefits of drinking and ignore the long-term problems it can cause.

3. Negative thinking can lead to drinking. Unpleasant thoughts and emotions can also lead to drinking. Some of these thoughts are about hopelessness or about negative self-worth. Examples are self-doubt, guilt, and anger. Negative thoughts are indirect triggers. They set up a chain of events that can lead to drinking.

What to Do?

Your thoughts lead to actions. Sometimes those thoughts go through your head so quickly that you believe you are acting without thinking. The idea of this next skill is to slow down the whole process so that you have more control over your

Figure 7.2
Thoughts That Can Trigger Drinking

thoughts and your actions. An important step in interrupting drinking chains is to recognize your thoughts in trigger situations. You have already listed many of your own triggers (see Chapter 2). Among these triggers you will find some dangerous thoughts.

Remember the behavior chain (refer back to Figure 2.1 in Chapter 2).

Imagine your dangerous thoughts as tripping off an alarm—a blinking red light in your head, indicating that it's time to deal with the trigger in a way that will avoid drinking. Your therapist will teach you the following ways to manage your dangerous thoughts.

1. a) You feel the "urge" to drink. Write down the positive thoughts you have about alcohol when you experience this urge (e.g., "ummm . . . a cold beer is so inviting!").
   b) Challenge the positive thoughts about alcohol with a replacement thought (e.g. "Beer is a toxin. I can't have just one.")

2. a) You feel the "urge" to drink. Write down a thought about positive consequences of drinking (e.g., "A cold wine spritzer would quench my thirst").
   b) Challenge and replace: "Think through the drink" (e.g., "Yes, it might taste good and quench my thirst at first, but I can't have just one, and so I will get drunk, neglect the kids, my husband will get angry, I will end up passed out on the couch and tomorrow I will feel ashamed and the kids will have this as a role model and a memory they don't deserve. And besides, alcohol only seems to quench thirst—it actually makes people even thirstier.")

3. a) You feel the "urge" to drink. Write down a negative thought that leads you to drink (e.g. "I've already been such a bad wife that my husband's family hates me. I might as well drink, what the hell. What's done is done.").
   b) Challenge and replace (e.g., "Yes, I have alienated my in-laws, but the truth is I don't really like them anyway and I won't let them have this much power over me. I won't drink because of them. The only way to clean up my act is to start by stopping drinking. My in-laws have nothing to do with this. I'm just using them as an excuse.")

Use the following worksheet to write down at least one personal example of each type of thought you have experienced that has led to drinking. Challenge each thought and come up with one that is more realistic and accurate.

Dealing With Alcohol-Related Thoughts

1. Direct, Positive Thoughts About Alcohol: (for example, an image of a cold glass of beer)

_____

_____

Challenge and Replace:

_____

_____

2. Thoughts about Positive Consequences of Alcohol: (for example, "A glass of wine will taste good")

_____

_____

Challenge and Replace:

_____

_____

3. Negative Thinking: (for example, "I'm such a loser, I might as well drink too")

_____

_____

Challenge and Replace:

_____

_____

Work with your therapist to identify at least one high-risk situation coming up in the next week. Write down ideas about how to handle this situation on the High-Risk Situations worksheet. Use the back of your self-recording card to record how you actually handled the anticipated situation, and write down any unexpected high-risk situations that may have arisen during the week.

High-Risk Situations

What high-risk situations do you think you may experience this week?

Situation 1:
How can you handle this situation?

a. _____

b. _____

c. _____

d. _____

Situation 2:
How can you handle this situation?

a. _____

b. _____

c. _____

d. _____

Situation 3:
How can you handle this situation?

a. _____

b. _____

c. _____

d. _____

Situation 4:
How can you handle this situation?

a. _____

b. _____

c. _____

d. _____

Homework

✎ Continue self-recording. Remember to use the back of your self-recording cards to write down the ways you handled your high-risk situations for the week.

✎ Continue to refer to your negative consequences card from Chapter 4 whenever you are faced with high-risk situations.

✎ Finish the I Want to Connect With People Who worksheet.

✎ Finish Making Connections worksheet and implement new ways for you to begin connecting with others.

✎ Start to develop a new thinking habit—finish filling out the Dealing With Alcohol-Related Thoughts worksheet.

✎ Review the information in this chapter.

Chapter 8

Session 8: Assertiveness Training / Drink Refusal

Goals

- To learn how to be assertive

- To practice drink refusal skills

Graphing Progress

In session, you will review the week with your therapist and together update your Alcohol Use and Urges Graph in Chapter 2 using the information from your most recently completed self-recording cards.

Recognizing Your Rights

Many people have interpersonal interactions that lead to unpleasant emotions. These bad emotions may then lead to drinking. Often, people have difficulty letting others know what they want. Few people learn the basics of speaking assertively. It seems obvious but it's not. Assertiveness means recognizing that each person has rights. It means that both you and the other person have rights. Assertiveness means that you are able to show respect to both the other person AND YOURSELF!

By rights, we mean the following:

- People have the right to make their feelings known in a way that does not hurt others.

- People have the right to make their opinions known to others.

- People have the right to request that another person change a behavior that is affecting others.

- People have the right to accept or reject anything that someone else says to them or requests of them.

Before starting assertiveness training, it is helpful to know about the different styles of communication. People generally choose one of three ways of responding to situations: passive, aggressive, or assertive.

Passive behavior is usually based on an underlying belief that you do not have the right to ask for what you want or that you do not deserve to have what you want. A person who consistently chooses a passive response and puts others' rights before his own most of the time may end up being "passive–aggressive," which can be considered a fourth way of responding. This means that he is angry but does not outwardly express anger. Instead, he may begin to talk maliciously behind someone's back instead of figuring out how to communicate directly with that person to get what he needs, or take on a project he doesn't think is fair, but somehow mess the project up by procrastinating, for instance—this is called being *passive-aggressive*. Sometimes a person can be passive for a while, building up resentment, and then eventually explode in an aggressive act.

Aggressive behavior is often associated with "losing your temper" and acting in an angry, mean way to bully someone into giving you want you want. Typically it does not result in your getting what you want, and often in fact has the opposite effect.

Assertive behavior is the "gold standard" and involves thinking about what you believe both you and the other party deserves and has a right to and then thinking about how best to choose an effective communication style to obtain what you want. Usually after an assertive response, you feel better about yourself and you haven't hurt anyone in the process.

People also have three different styles of asking something from others:

Passive people give up their rights whenever it appears conflict will erupt between what they and the other person wants. By not respecting their own rights, people who act passively often suffer from anxiety or resentment. These unpleasant emotions can be triggers for drinking. An example of someone acting passively is the person who really wants to do something but is afraid of the reaction that other people will have.

Aggressive people usually act to get their rights, but often ignore the rights of others. At first, they get what they want, but build up long-term problems with others. Over time, other people resent the aggressiveness and may retaliate. An example of aggressiveness is someone threatening another person to do something or else suffer some consequence.

Assertive people balance their rights with those of other people. They decide their goals and then work with others to achieve these goals. Usually, the most effective way to operate assertively is to state what you want while letting others know that you understand their position. The assertive person adapts what he says to the situation. By being respectful of the rights of all people, the assertive approach is the most effective one over time.

Review the chart Which Do You Do? (Table 8.1), and see if you can identify the responses you typically use. In session, you will be filling out the Assertiveness worksheet and role-playing your response to the situations.

Table 8.1 Which Do You Do?

Passive Behavior	Aggressive Behavior	Assertive Behavior
Self-denying ("Let him go first, even though I've been waiting longer.")	**Loses control of anger** ("These idiots had better give me what I want!!")	**Feels good about self** ("I stayed in control and I feel good about that.")
Inhibited ("I can't ask that—it may sound silly.")	**Chooses for others** ("Just do it my way and shut up.")	**Chooses for self** ("I am an adult; I can remain calm and ask for this.")
Hurt, anxious ("What if they don't like me?")	**Feels ashamed after losing control** ("I can never come back to this store.")	**Considers rights of self and others** ("I don't think I'm taking advantage. I have every right to ask this. It's fair to both of us.")
Allows others to choose for self		
Does not achieve desired goal ("Oh well . . . ")	**Does not achieve desired goal** ("I stomped out and now I still can't return this stained shirt.")	**Usually achieves desired goal** ("Yes!!")
Does not feel worthy of desired goal ("Oh well . . . ")	**Does not consider others' rights** ("Just give me what I want!")	**Takes responsibility** ("It doesn't matter if life is unfair—I'm the one who loses if I don't try to take care of myself.")
Resentment grows ("Why doesn't anybody see how hard I work?")	**Hurts others**	
Often results in explosive aggression ("I'VE HAD ENOUGH!!!")	**Is quite unpopular**	**Feels worthy of her own rights** ("I do deserve this!")
Talks behind others' backs (passive-aggressive)	**Feels out of control and stressed**	**Thinks about how to word things** ("Let's see, getting angry won't help. Take a deep breath and figure out how to say this in an effective way . . . ")
Gossips (passive-aggressive)		
Complains a lot (passive-aggressive)		**Expressive**
Whines about unfair situation (passive-aggressive)		**Feels calmer and in control**
Does not take responsibility ("They are so unfair . . . no one sees that . . . ")		
Feels helpless and depressed		
Does not command respect		

Assertiveness

Record your behavior in two situations in which assertive behavior may have been helpful. In the following columns, describe the situation, describe your response, and label your response as passive, aggressive, or assertive.

Situation	Your Response	Passive? Aggressive? Assertive?

Speaking Assertively

Many people have interpersonal problems that lead to unpleasant emotions. These bad emotions then lead to drinking. Often, people have difficulty letting others know what they want. Few people learn the basics of speaking assertively. Assertiveness training can help you learn how to act more effectively. There are several situations in which assertiveness may be helpful:

- frustrating and anger-inducing situations

- making requests

- refusing requests

- giving criticism

- receiving criticism

Guidelines for Speaking Assertively

Your Thoughts

- Think about how you want the situation to turn out.

- Remind yourself that getting angry will not achieve desired goals and you will feel ashamed after.

- Remind yourself that doing nothing also will not achieve your goals and you'll feel frustrated.

- Try to think about the situation from the other person's position.

- Recognize the other person's rights. If the person feels respected, he will be more likely to respect you.

- Think about how to word your request.

- Talk yourself through it.

Your Feelings

- Understand what you are feeling.

- You are allowed to feel as angry as you want, but you acting on those feelings impulsively without the filter of assertiveness will probably backfire.

- Take a deep cleansing breath, or use relaxation breathing skills (from Session 6) to focus and be calm.

- When you feel really angry, take a time-out.

Your Actions

- Take action before you are too afraid to act, or so angry you can barely contain yourself.

- Don't go in looking for a fight—assume the person wants to help resolve the issue and approach the issue in a calm, problem-solving way, not in an emotional, adversarial way.

- Begin with a positive statement and balance the negative with positive, so that the other person does not feel attacked.

- Speak up clearly and in a respectful but clear tone. Don't apologize.

- Look the other person in the eye, but keep your nonverbals relaxed and not aggressive. This tells the other person that you are confident but respectful.

- Use guidelines for good communication:

  - Be polite.
  - Avoid blaming and sentences that begin with "you," which make the other person feel attacked.
  - Keep your voice tone pleasant.

- Clearly state what you want and why.

- Request a specific change. Vague requests do not work because the other person is not clear about what you want.

- Be firm but polite in your answers to requests made by the other person.

Steps to Communicating Assertively

1. Start with something nice.

2. Calmly explain your position without blaming others.

   Instead of, *"Your store sold me a defective shirt with a stain on it and your return policy is ridiculous"* say, *"I bought this shirt here a few weeks ago and didn't notice until I went to wear it yesterday for the first time that it has a stain on it which must have been there when I bought it. Unfortunately, it's past the return date according to the policy but since I haven't worn it I would like to exchange it for a similar shirt with no stain."*

3. Start with an "I" statement whenever possible.

4. Explain calmly what you are upset about.

5. Make a specific request for change.

6. No Grand Slam plays. Instead of storming out, be politely persistent. (*"I see you're busy. May I speak with the manager, please?"*)

How to Refuse a Drink

The ability to refuse drinks is much more difficult than it appears. It is another weapon in your arsenal of skills to stay sober. In the session, you are going to practice ways of refusing or turning down drinks so that you can gain control in these tough situations.

One-third of problem drinkers have a slip because of pressure from others. Refusing offers of drinks is harder than most people think. It takes special skills to say no to drinks.

Offers of drinks come in many forms. Sometimes friends or coworkers put pressure on you to join in their drinking. Other times the pressure comes from family members. Sometimes you may be concerned about what others will think if you refuse the drink.

Some people are easier to refuse than others. Some will politely accept your first refusal. Others may get pushy.

Drink refusal is an important assertiveness skill. The foundation of assertiveness skills is respect for your own needs. Remember that individuals who encourage you to drink are pushers—and must be discouraged politely but firmly. Be firm without getting aggressive. By using the following skills, you can refuse a drink without coming on too strong.

How to refuse drinks:

- "No" or "no thank you" should be the first thing you say. Starting with "no" makes it tougher for the pusher to try to manipulate you.

- Look the person in the eye when you speak. Eye contact makes you come across as firm. Not looking the other person in the eye tells him that you are not sure about what you are saying.

- Speak clearly and in a serious tone. Your manner should say that you mean business.

- You have a right to say no. You want to stay sober. It is your life that you are protecting. Do not feel guilty. You have a right to say no and be in control.

- Suggest alternatives. If someone is offering a drink, ask for something nonalcoholic. If someone is asking you to get into a risky situation, suggest something else that is not risky.

- Change the subject to a new topic of conversation.

- Ask the person not to continue offering you a drink. Someone who is pushing you to drink is not respecting your rights. Ask him to leave you alone.

- Know your bottom line. You are saying no out of respect for yourself. If the person keeps pushing, use your problem-solving skills. Remember, you can leave, get the person to leave, or get help from others.

- And finally . . . practice, practice, practice!

These skills are difficult to use in a real situation. Social pressure is one of the most difficult problems that people face. Many people you know drink or expect you to drink. They will have a difficult time accepting the change.

Think of different situations you may face. Develop some strategies for handling each. Practice with your therapist how you would use these skills. Practice at home—use the mirror. Practice in real situations when you feel ready. Remember to reward yourself for doing the right thing!

Drink Refusal Examples

You're at your brother's house on Christmas Day. It's a special occasion; you are with family and friends. Your brother says, "How about a beer?" You say, "No thanks, I'd like a soda though."

A group of your friends stop or approach you at a party and offer you a drink. They say, "Hey Jill, how about a glass of wine?" You say, "No thanks, I'm not drinking." They say, "Oh come on! One drink won't hurt. What kind of friend are you?" or "What's the matter? Are you too good to drink with us?" You say, "I'll just take a selzer with lemon, thanks."

High-Risk Situations for the Week

Work with your therapist to identify at least one high-risk situation coming up in the next week. Write down ideas about how to handle this situation on the High-Risk Situations worksheet. Use the back of your self-recording card to record how you actually handled the anticipated situation, and write down any unexpected high-risk situations that may have arisen during the week.

High-Risk Situations

What high-risk situations do you think you may experience this week?

Situation 1:
How can you handle this situation?

a. _____

b. _____

c. _____

d. _____

Situation 2:
How can you handle this situation?

a. _____

b. _____

c. _____

d. _____

Situation 3:
How can you handle this situation?

a. _____

b. _____

c. _____

d. _____

Situation 4:
How can you handle this situation?

a. _____

b. _____

c. _____

d. _____

Homework

✎ Continue self-recording. Remember to use the back of your self-recording cards to write down the ways you handled your high-risk situations for the week.

✎ Determine a situation during the next week in which you will be offered alcohol. Practice your refusal scenes twice daily.

✎ Continue employing self-control procedures.

✎ Implement 2 strategies to connect with others (see Making Connections worksheet in Chapter 7).

✎ Identify 2 situations during the week to use your assertiveness skills. Write on back of self-monitoring card what happened.

✎ Review the information in this chapter.

Chapter 9

Session 9: Anger Management Part I / Relapse Prevention Part I: Seemingly Irrelevant Decisions

Goals

- To learn how to manage your anger

- To start learning about relapses and how to avoid them by discussing the impact of seemingly irrelevant decisions on your drinking

Graphing Progress

In session, you will review the week with your therapist and together update your Alcohol Use and Urges Graph in Chapter 2 using the information from your most recently completed self-recording cards.

Anger Management

Sometimes we find ourselves "flying off the handle"—losing our temper when someone or an unfair situation makes us mad. Some people tend to be "reactive" rather than "proactive."

For instance, imagine a State Department negotiator losing her temper at what she perceives as an unfair decision. Does she start to scream and cry? Does she yell and throw things? No, typically she remains "cool headed" and not reactive. She still feels angry, of course, but she doesn't act on her anger in a destructive way.

Now imagine a person in front of you in line at the department store. She has lost her temper because the cashier won't accept a return without a receipt. She starts to scream and swear at the cashier, then stomps out of the store yelling, "That's the last time I shop here!" Everyone on line just shakes their heads and goes on with their business. The woman did not get what she wanted and for the rest of the day felt embarrassed and ashamed about her behavior in the store.

Which way do you want to behave? Which way do you think commands more respect from others, and more importantly, more self-respect? Losing your temper is usually not productive. Just because someone may try to provoke you into anger or into an argument doesn't mean you have to accept! You have the choice and the right to not get angry! Instead you can choose to handle anything that comes your way in a self-respecting, nonreactive way.

Use the Anger Triggers worksheet provided in this chapter to identify what types of situations are anger triggers for you (see first line of each category for examples). Then pick a trigger from the Anger Triggers worksheet and complete an Anger Behavior Chain worksheet for these triggers as follows (see Figure 9.1 for a completed example).

Thoughts/Feelings Column: Remember back to the last time you faced this trigger and write down what thoughts were going through your head (write down the actual thoughts). Also write down what feelings you experienced. Be specific—"angry" is good but not enough: Is it a physical sensation, a tightening sensation in your chest, a feeling that your heart is pounding, or a "tense" feeling all over?

Response Column: Write down what "response" you typically have in response to that trigger and those thoughts/feelings. For example, the last time you responded to that particular trigger did you scream? Did your voice shake? Did you become violent—if so, what exactly did you do? Did you roll your eyes, walk away, and then later take your anger out on someone else?

Positive Consequences Column: Write down what the short-term positive consequences were of your response. Typically this involves release of anger and temporary satisfaction or relief of tension. Also try to identify a few long-term positive consequences (there may not be any of these).

Negative Consequences Column: Write down the short-term and long-term negative consequences. Typical short-term negative consequences would be the following: feeling embarrassed after screaming, feeling regret about reacting so strongly, not achieving desired goal, others thinking you're "crazy," feeling out of control, having uncomfortable physical sensations, etc. Long-term negative consequences of an angry response might include the following: cumulative damage to a relationship after repeated angry episodes, eroded lack of trust by others, and medical problems in cardiovascular and vasculatory system due to chronic release of excess stress hormones.

You will need to develop new ways of dealing with those triggers, challenging angry thoughts, and calming down without the use of alcohol. One way to calm down is by taking a "time out." You will learn about this technique in the next session. You can also find alternatives to angry responses in the sections on assertiveness training (Session 8), how to manage strong negative emotions (Session 6), and calming down before proceeding with problem solving (Session 10).

Anger Behavior Chain

Anger Trigger	Thoughts/feelings	Response	Positive Consequences	Negative consequences
Received a child support check 1 week late and I notice that he deducted a toy he bought for our child.	"What a jerk! He is not allowed to do that!" "Now he'll start deducting whatever he buys and I won't have enough to pay the bills" "I need to give him a piece of my mind!" Anger, rage, burning up	Call ex-husband, leave screaming message	Momentarily relieved	Children say "Mom, you're crazy" Ex-husband plays taped message for the judge as evidence that kids are right Feel ashamed Situation not resolved Still angry
Same trigger	"What a jerk! He is not allowed to do that!" "Now he'll start deducting whatever he buys and I won't have enough to pay the bills" "If I call him I'll just leave a screaming message and I know he keeps those tapes to use against me" "Of course I'm angry, he's an expert at pressing my buttons. I won't let myself suffer anger because of him" "I'll call my lawyer in the morning, so this doesn't happen again because it's not fair." "The toy only cost $25—I can afford that and it's for Jimmy" "I feel sorry for him—doesn't he have anything better to think about in life, than trying to push my buttons" "I'm angry and I know that's normal but I don't want to feel angry. I'm going to swim some laps until I feel better"	Swim laps Take a walk	Feel less angry Proud of self—didn't lose control No screaming message taped to use against me Ex doesn't have satisfaction of having gotten to me Lawyer will help resolve situation Got some exercise	Still feel a bit like screaming at him, frustrating

Figure 9.1

Example of Completed Anger Behavior Chain, illustrating an ineffective response versus a more effective response to the same anger trigger.

Anger Triggers

Environmental (places, things)
stuck in traffic not moving on highway for an hour

Interpersonal (people)
spouse interrupting during an argument, won't let me finish a sentence, and just keeps
repeating same thing over and over

Emotions/Thoughts
anxious about being late for work when stuck in traffic
"this stupid stalled bus is making us all sit here—what is it doing in the middle of the
road? Why can't the traffic police resolve this?"

Physical
In withdrawal from alcohol

Figure 9.2
Example of Completed Anger Triggers Worksheet

Anger Triggers

Environmental (places, things)

_____

_____

_____

_____

_____

Interpersonal (people)

_____

_____

_____

_____

_____

Emotions/Thoughts

_____

_____

_____

_____

_____

Physical

_____

_____

_____

_____

_____

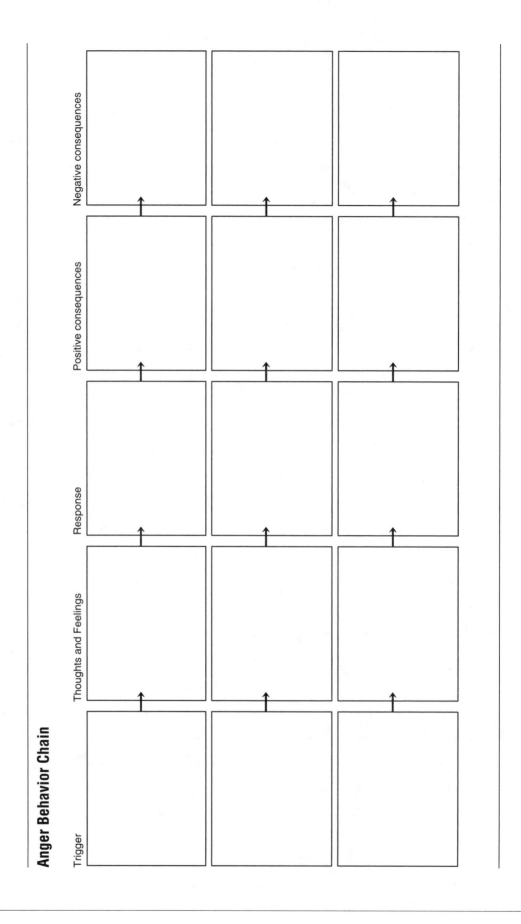

Anger Behavior Chain

Trigger   Thoughts and Feelings   Response   Positive consequences   Negative consequences

Many of the ordinary choices that you make every day seem to have nothing to do with drinking. Although these choices do not appear to be related to drinking, often you will find that small decisions lead to trigger situations. This is the domino effect of small decisions. One decision leads to another, which leads to another, and so on. A number of small decisions may bring you closer to a high-risk situation. Put together, the decisions that set up drinking are what we call "seemingly irrelevant decisions."

Jeff's Seemingly Irrelevant Decisions

Think about this story and try to identify Jeff's seemingly irrelevant decisions that led to his final decision to drink some beer. Underline each one of the choice points where Jeff could have made a different decision that would have taken him away from a dangerous situation:

> *Jeff is on his way home from work and hasn't had a drink in 5 months. He's gotten to the point where he catches himself not thinking about alcohol for 2 to 3 days at a time. It's hot outside and he wants to get home, but today there's a 10 million dollar lottery and wants to stop to buy a couple of lottery tickets on the way home. He pulls into the liquor store/bar he used to frequent; he knows they sell lottery tickets there. He buys the tickets and is about to turn around and walk out when he hears his name being called. He looks behind him and sees Rich, an old drinking buddy, waving him over to the bar. He walks over to say hi, and finds an ice-cold beer that Rich has ordered for him, waiting at the counter. Before he can stop himself, he downs the beer and orders another.*

You may be able to see that Jeff made a series of decisions that led to his final decision to drink. For each one of the choices, Jeff could have made a different decision that would have led him away from a risky situation. Did he really need to buy his lottery ticket at a bar? Did he have to walk over to his old drinking buddy, or could he have just waved hello to him? Could he have said "no" to himself about the first beer? Jeff made a series of decisions. Each one of the decisions contributed to his finally drinking.

For more practice, do the following exercise: Georgia's Seemingly Irrelevant Decisions.

Georgia's Seemingly Irrelevant Decisions

Read the following scenario, and underline the seemingly irrelevant decisions Georgia made that were high-risk and led to her slip.

Georgia decided to make a gourmet dinner for her and her husband and invited another couple to join them. She felt good about being abstinent from alcohol in the last two months and did not want to drink with dinner. However, she knew that the husband and wife in the other couple both liked wine and that red wine would go well with the menu she had planned. She also felt it would not be fair of her to deprive the others of alcohol. Therefore, she asked her husband to buy a couple of bottles of good red wine for the company. During the dinner, she felt comfortable not drinking. Her husband and their friends finished one bottle of wine and started the second. When Georgia was cleaning up in the kitchen after her friends had left, she looked at the almost full bottle of wine and decided it would feel good to have one glass and that she would then stop drinking. She had a glass of wine and then went on to have several more glasses, finishing the bottle.

Your Seemingly Irrelevant Decisions

People often think of themselves as victims: "Things just seemed to happen in such a way that I ended up in a high-risk situation and then had a drink—I could not help it." They think things happen to them without realizing that many little decisions get them into trouble. That is because many of the decisions do not actually seem to involve drinking at the time. Each choice you make may take you just a little closer to drinking. But after you've been sober for awhile, it's hard to make the connection between a choice that doesn't seem related to alcohol at the moment and later trouble.

The best solution is to think about every choice you have to make, no matter how seemingly irrelevant it is to drinking. By thinking ahead about each possible option you have and where each of them may lead, you can anticipate dangers that may lie along certain paths. It may feel awkward at first to have to consider everything so carefully, but after awhile, it becomes second nature and happens automatically, without much effort.

By paying more attention to the decision-making process, you'll have a greater chance to interrupt the chain of decisions that could lead to a relapse. This is important because it's much easier to stop the process early, before you wind up in a high-risk situation, than later, when you're in a situation that's harder to handle and where you may be exposed to a number of triggers.

So, when you have a decision to make, choose a low-risk option, to avoid putting yourself in a risky situation. If you have to make a high-risk decision, plan ahead to protect yourself while in the high-risk situation.

Seemingly Irrelevant Decisions

Safe Choices

_____

_____

_____

_____

_____

_____

_____

_____

_____

_____

_____

_____

_____

_____

_____

_____

_____

Risky Choices

_____

_____

_____

_____

_____

_____

_____

_____

_____

_____

_____

_____

_____

_____

_____

_____

_____

High-Risk Situations for the Week

Work with your therapist to identify at least one high-risk situation coming up in the next week. Write down ideas about how to handle this situation on the High-Risk Situations worksheet. Use the back of your self-recording card to record how you actually handled the anticipated situation, and write down any unexpected high-risk situations that may have arisen during the week.

High-Risk Situations

What high-risk situations do you think you may experience this week?

Situation 1:
How can you handle this situation?

a. _____

b. _____

c. _____

d. _____

Situation 2:
How can you handle this situation?

a. _____

b. _____

c. _____

d. _____

Situation 3:
How can you handle this situation?

a. _____

b. _____

c. _____

d. _____

Situation 4:
How can you handle this situation?

a. _____

b. _____

c. _____

d. _____

Homework

✎ Continue self-recording. Remember to use the back of your self-recording cards to write down the ways you handled your high-risk situations for the week.

✎ Continue implementing strategies for connecting with others.

✎ Finish Anger Triggers worksheet.

✎ Finish Anger Behavior Chain worksheet.

✎ Use new skills on anger management this week if situation arises and write on back of self-recording card what happened.

✎ Think about a decision you have made recently or are about to make. The decision could involve any aspect of your life, such as your job, recreational activities, friends, or family. Identify safe choices that might decrease your risk for relapse and record these on the Seemingly Irrelevant Decisions worksheet.

✎ Review the information in this chapter.

Chapter 10

Session 10: Anger Management
Part II / Problem Solving / Relapse
Prevention Part II

Goals

- To use "time-outs" as an alternative response to anger triggers

- To practice self-calming in preparation for problem solving

- To learn how to problem solve effectively

- To identify warning signs for relapse and devise plans for handling them when they come up

Graphing Progress

In session, you will review the week with your therapist and together update your Alcohol Use and Urges and Graph in Chapter 2 using the information from your most recently completed self-recording cards.

Anger Management Part II: Time-Out

Last session started talking about how to deal with feeling angry. One good strategy is to use a "time-out" to help you calm down. "Time-out" means taking a break from a situation where you are getting angry or tense. You can also use this method if you are starting to feel anxious or depressed. Use a time-out to relax, think, cool down, and avoid being unreasonable, or violent. Remember, it takes two people to make an argument. Just because someone else is angry, doesn't mean you have to be. You are a separate person. It is your choice to engage in arguments; it is your choice how to react to an unfair situation.

Here are some tips for taking a time-out.

Things to Tell the Other Person

If you are with someone when you choose to take a time-out, you need to tell the other person:

1. What you are going to do

2. Where you are going (e.g., next room, to a friend's house)

3. When you will return (certain number of minutes/hours)

Example: "I'm going to take a walk to cool off and I'll be back in an hour."

Steps to Taking a Time-Out

Below are the steps involved in taking a time-out:

Tell the other person that you are feeling tense and need some time to relax and think. It is important to communicate that you are not trying to avoid the problems and that you will be willing to talk about them later when you feel more relaxed and reasonable.

Get away from the person and the situation. It is best to leave the area altogether.

Do not drive a vehicle, use drugs, use a gun, or drink alcohol during a "time-out."

Calm yourself physically and mentally. Use a combination of physical and mental exercises that are nonaggressive. Concentrate on your breathing. Identify negative affect thoughts. Practice challenging and replacing them with positive self-talk.

Give yourself time to relax and get control of yourself. When we get angry or anxious, our heart rate increases, blood pressure rises, blood sugar level rises, and certain other chemicals increase in our bodies. It takes time for our body to get back to normal. Give yourself at least 20 min and preferably, 45 min to an hour before returning to the situation.

Repeat, if necessary, the time-out procedure until there is no risk of getting out of control.

Once you're calm, you can use your assertiveness skills to handle the upsetting situation.

Time-Out Do's and Don'ts

Some Things to Do During a Time-Out

Do: Practice positive self-talk. For example:

- *As long as I keep my cool, I'm in control of myself.*

- *I'm the only person who can make myself angry or calm myself down.*

- *It's time to relax and slow things down.*

- *It's impossible to control other people and situations. The only thing I can control is myself and how I express my feelings.*

- *It's nice to have other people's love and approval, but even without it, I can still accept and like myself.*

Do: Go for a walk, jog, run, or swim to help work off some of the energy.

Do: Think of constructive solutions to the problem.

Do: Make use of your positive social connections—talk to a good friend.

Do: Check in when you return home.

Do: Let yourself have a good cry if you want to.

Do: Let yourself feel sad if you need to. Then, let it go and allow yourself to feel hopeful.

Some Things to Avoid During a Time Out

Do not...use alcohol. You will just create a new set of problems, and alcohol increases hostility, anxiety, and depression. Alcohol makes it impossible to gain self-control and self-respect.

Do not...talk with people who will feed your anger.

Do not...go to places where you have used alcohol in the past.

Do not...drive while angry. It is not only self-destructive, but dangerous to others as well.

Do not...use any weapons.

Do not...justify your anger or think about how wrong the other person is.

Do not . . . think about ways to control aspects of the situation you can't.

Do not . . . let yourself get sucked in to anxious thoughts—let them come and go.

Do not . . . tell yourself you're crazy for feeling this way. You're not.

Problem Solving as a General Coping Skill

Problem-solving skills are a very important part of changing behavior and learning to negotiate changes. This session focuses on using problem solving as a general coping skill.

Types of Coping Strategies

There are at least two types of coping strategies that people tend to use.

Emotion-focused coping is when one gets caught up in the negative emotions associated with a life problem. Anger, sadness, frustration are common emotions that one focuses on and then often feels the need to escape from (i.e., by drinking to "feel numb" or "make the problem go away"). This type of coping is often not effective and can in fact increase distress and make things worse.

Problem-focused coping is when one acknowledges and tolerates difficult emotions, but puts them aside in order to deal with the actual problem in a relatively nonemotional, rational way. This type of coping is generally much more effective in resolving difficult situations and in defusing distress.

Self-Calming

In order to problem solve effectively, you will need to be in a calm and rational state. If you feel overwhelmed by emotion in response to a particular problem, you will need to calm yourself down before attempting problem solving. Strategies for self-calming include:

- using relaxation breathing (introduced in Session 6)—taking a deep breath from your stomach every 10 seconds or so for 20 min

- taking a walk outside for 20 min breathing deeply

- counting to ten, taking a few deep breaths, and telling yourself that acting on these emotions will be counterproductive

- meditating

Can you identify other strategies for calming yourself down?

_____

_____

_____

Problem-Solving Method

Everyone has faced a big problem that seemed impossible to conquer. Some people get lost in the problem and do not find a solution. Other people go through a method that helps them solve it.

There is a method that many people use to solve difficult problems. This method is easy to understand. You will need to go through a number of steps to solve a problem. As with any new skill, you will need to practice using this method to solve problems. The more you use it, the easier it gets. At first, you will find the method a little awkward. But the more you use it, the more natural it will seem to you.

The skills presented here can be applied to any part of your life. You have already used some of these skills when coping with urges and planning for difficult situations.

The problem-solving method has seven steps:

1. *Gather information*: Think about the problem situation. Who is involved? When does it happen? Exactly what takes place? What effect does this have on you? What happens before the problem (the antecedents)? What keeps the problem going (the consequences)? Where does it occur? How does the problem affect you?

2. *Define the problem*: What is the goal that you would like to achieve? Be clear and specific. Many people get into trouble at this step because they select very vague goals. Define your goal as something that can be counted. The more specific and real you make the problem, the easier it will be to solve.

3. *Brainstorm for alternatives*: This can be a fun step. The goal of this step is to build a long list of possible solutions. The first rule of brainstorming is that no idea is too silly or dumb. Try to think about any and every possible solution to the problem. Do not think about how good or bad each idea is—that will come later. By not evaluating the ideas as they come, you will

be more creative in thinking of solutions. Make as long a list as you can. The number of ideas is more important than their quality.

4. *Now, consider the consequences of each*: For each of your alternatives, list the positive and negative consequences. Think about the short-term and long-term results of each solution. Ask yourself: What things can you reasonably expect to happen? What will be the positive consequences? What will be the negative consequences? Which consequences will happen right away? Which consequences will happen later? How can you combine different alternatives?

5. *Decide*: Which of the alternatives is the most likely to achieve the goal you set in Step 2? Look for the solution (or solutions) that have the best balance of consequences.

6. *Do it!* The best plan in the world is useless if you do not put into action. Try it out.

7. *Evaluate*: Check out how the plan is working. Which parts work best? Which parts can you improve? Fix what can be fixed.

In addition, reward yourself for taking action! You have done something to help yourself.

Problem-Solving Example

Problem definition:

- Background: *Susan's live-in boyfriend is less responsible with money than she is, and she often finds herself paying the household bills. She is developing resentment toward her boyfriend, since he regularly promises to pay but then uses his money on his personal expenses instead.*

- Specific problem situation: *Susan wants to find a different way to deal with this situation.*

Brainstorming for alternatives:

- *Keep trying to ask him for money when she needs it to pay bills and hope he changes*

- *Open a joint checking account, and plan for each of them to have certain amount of paycheck direct deposited into that account, which Susan will use for the household bills*

■ *Ask boyfriend to take over the bill paying*

■ *Hire an accountant or bookkeeper to handle all household finances*

Decision making (choosing the most effective alternative):

■ Evaluate the positive and negative consequences of each possible alternative (see Figure 10.1.)

■ Choose the alternative with the best payoff, solving the problem while maximizing positive consequences and minimizing negatives.

Problem-Solving Worksheet

	Pros	Cons
a. Keep doing the same	+ Familiar + Boyfriend not mad	− Resentment grows − Possible break-up of relationship − Unfair to Susan
b. Open joint checking	+ Fair to both + Susan doesn't have to ask boyfriend for money + Reduced resentment	− Need to deal with paperwork for direct deposit change − Need to open bank account − Susan still paying the bills
c. Ask boyfriend to take over bills	+ Susan reduces resentment + Susan doesn't have to ask for money	− Boyfriend probably not capable − Damage to credit history − Bills not paid − Resentment eventually increased on both sides
d. Hire accountant	+ Less burden for Susan + Less resentment of boyfriend	− Expensive − Someone else knows all personal business

Figure 10.1

Example of Completed Problem-Solving Worksheet

Problem-Solving Worksheet

Pick a problem that has come up in the course of treatment so far and practice solving it using the methods just described.

1. Gather Information: _____

2. Problem Definition: _____

3. Brainstorming for Solutions and Listing of Pros and Cons:

Solution	Pros (short and long term)	Cons (short and long term)
a.		
b.		
c.		
d.		
e.		

4. Pick solution(s): _____

5. Implement the solution for a period of time.

6. Reevaluate the solution—Did it work? _____

If not, do problem solving again.

Warning Signs of Relapse

Until now we have talked about remaining abstinent from alcohol. The goal is for you to stop drinking completely. We have focused on skills that help you remain abstinent in the long run. However, we do know that many people who want to stay sober may have difficulties at times and may experience a slip or relapse. The best skill is to be aware of warning signs and handle them without drinking. However, people do have slips, and while we do not want this to happen, we believe it is important to be ready for possible slips.

It may seem pessimistic to discuss drinking when you're not, but we like to think about relapse prevention the way we think about fire prevention. For fire prevention, we look at possible dangers in our homes, schools, and workplaces. We remain aware of possible trouble: something flammable near a heat source or strange smoke. And though we don't want or even expect a fire, we make sure to have a plan in place to minimize the damage and/or escape if a fire occurs. We know where the fire extinguishers are and how to contact the fire department, and we have an evacuation plan established. Similarly, we should remain aware of signs of trouble about possible drinking, which we call warning signs for relapse. You and your therapist will generate a plan to deal with these warning signs to help prevent relapse. Next session, you will generate a plan to deal with slips and relapses to use in the event that they occur.

Identifying Warning Signs

Warning signs might be changes in the way you think and interact or changes in habits. You have learned many new behaviors. Through dedication, these behaviors can become everyday habits. Changes in these new habits may signal trouble. Look out for old habits, especially ones that led to trouble in the past. Look for changes in mood, people you associate with, places you go to, ways you handle problems, and routines. Be alert for changes in the way you think about alcohol, yourself, or things around you. All these things could signal the possibility of a slip.

Think back to your last slip. What were the signals of trouble? Remember the few days before the slip. What things had changed? Look for changes in actions or thoughts that may have warned you of trouble. These old signals are ones you should watch for.

Use the Identifying and Managing Relapse worksheet to list the thoughts, feelings, and behaviors that you experienced before your last lapse. These are your warning signs. You will talk about how to handle these warning signs later on in the session.

Identifying and Managing Relapse Warning Signs

Warning signs

How to handle warning signs

1. _____

_____

2. _____

_____

3. _____

_____

4. _____

_____

5. _____

_____

1. _____

_____

2. _____

_____

3. _____

_____

4. _____

_____

5. _____

_____

Managing Warning Signs for Relapse

Your therapist is going to help you prepare to face situations that will occur after treatment ends. Having a list of warning signs for relapses does not necessarily mean that you will be aware of them as warning signs when they actually occur—remember the discussion of seemingly irrelevant decisions from Chapter 9.

Review the relapse warning signs that you listed on the Identifying and Managing Relapse worksheet, and make a *plan* for what to do for each sign if it should occur. Write down the plans in the spaces provided on the worksheet.

High-Risk Situations for the Week

Work with your therapist to identify at least one high-risk situation coming up in the next week. Write down ideas about how to handle this situation on the High-Risk Situations worksheet. Use the back of your self-recording card to record how you actually handled the anticipated situation, and write down any unexpected high-risk situations that may have arisen during the week.

High-Risk Situations

What high-risk situations do you think you may experience this week?

Situation 1:
How can you handle this situation?

a. _____

b. _____

c. _____

d. _____

Situation 2:
How can you handle this situation?

a. _____

b. _____

c. _____

d. _____

Situation 3:
How can you handle this situation?

a. _____

b. _____

c. _____

d. _____

Situation 4:
How can you handle this situation?

a. _____

b. _____

c. _____

d. _____

Homework

✎ Continue self-recording. Remember to use the back of your self-recording cards to write down the ways you handled your high-risk situations for the week.

✎ Practice self-calming strategies.

✎ Complete one problem-solving exercise.

✎ Complete the Identifying and Managing Relapse Warning Signs worksheet.

✎ Review the information in this chapter.

Chapter 11   *Session 11: Relapse Prevention Part III*

Goals

- To learn about slips and relapses

- To learn ways of handling slips and relapses

- To come up with a plan for handling slips and relapses

Graphing Progress

In session, you will review the week with your therapist and together update your Alcohol Use and Urges and Graph in Chapter 2 using the information from your most recently completed self-recording cards.

Slips and Relapses

Slips can be very challenging. Even using your best skills you may still have difficulties. It will be easier for you in the long run if you don't, but it is possible that you will eventually take a drink, despite your best efforts. Sometimes people who slip give up on their abstinence goals and head back to drinking. If drinking occurs, it is important to realize that one drink does not have to inevitably lead to a full-blown relapse.

A person who slips can think of it in three ways:

1. The slip is a mistake that shouldn't be repeated. This is considered a lapse if the person does not continue drinking.

2. The slip is an opportunity to learn about something risky. The person should think of different ways to handle the situation in the future. This is considered a "prolapse" if the person does not continue drinking, but learns a lesson for the future.

3. The slip is a disaster that shows that the person is hopeless. People who see the slip in this way think, "I have blown it. I will never succeed. I will just give up." Giving up and returning to drinking is called a relapse.

The third way of thinking is the worst choice. Slips are like falling off a bicycle. The fall may hurt, but you should get back on the bicycle and keep riding. You may feel rotten about the slip, but you can get back to remaining sober. The slip may even be an opportunity to learn about a difficult situation.

Handling Slips and Relapses

Looking for and thinking about warning signs help to prevent a slip. However, even people who work hard to remain abstinent may find themselves in an overwhelming situation. While you should work hard and expect to not take another drink, we believe you should be prepared for the possibility of a slip.

If you should take a drink, you have choices. As discussed previously, there are three different ways to think about the drink. You could think of it as a mistake (a slip), a mistake from which you learn something (a prolapse), or as a hopeless disaster (a relapse). The goal is never to have a relapse.

A drink does not have to become a relapse. If you ever have a drink, you should try to make it turn out to be a slip or prolapse. If you have a drink, remember the following:

1. **Don't panic**. One drink does not have to lead to an extended binge or a return to uncontrolled drinking.

2. **Stop, look, and listen**. Stop the ongoing flow of events and look and listen to what is happening. The lapse should be seen as a warning signal that the client or couple is in trouble. The lapse is like a flat tire—it is time to pull off the road to deal with the situation.

3. **Be aware of the abstinence violation effect**. Once you have a drink you may have thoughts such as, "I blew it," or "All our efforts were a waste," or "As long as I've blown it, I might as well keep drinking," or "My willpower has failed, I have no control," or "I'm addicted, and once I drink my body will take over." These thoughts might be accompanied by feelings of anger or guilt. It is crucial to dispute these thoughts immediately.

4. **Renew your commitment**. After a lapse, it is easy to feel discouraged and to want to give up. Think back over the reasons why you decided to change your drinking in the first place; look at your decisional matrix and think about all the positive long-term benefits of abstinence and the long-term problems associated with continued drinking.

5. **Decide on a course of action**. At a minimum, this should include:

   - Getting out of the drinking situation.
   - Waiting at least 2 h before having a second drink.
   - Engaging in some activity during those 2 h that would help avoid continued drinking. The activity might be a pleasurable one, or reviewing materials from treatment, or talking over the lapse with someone who could be helpful, or calling your therapist.

6. **Review the situation leading up to the lapse**. Don't blame yourself for what happened. By focusing on your own failings, you will feel guiltier and blame yourself more. Ask yourself, what events led up to the slip? What were the main triggers? Were there any early warning signs? Did you try to deal with these constructively? If not, why? Was your motivation weakened by fatigue, social pressure, or depression? Once you have analyzed the slip, think about what changes you need to make to avoid future slips.

7. **Ask for help**. Make it easier on yourself by asking someone to help you either by encouraging you, giving you advice, distracting you, or engaging in some alternative activity with you. If you had a flat tire and your spare tire also was flat, you'd have to get help—a slip is the same situation.

Using the worksheet provided, write down some ideas for handling slips or relapses should they occur.

Plan for Handling Slips and Relapses

Immediate plans to prevent the slip from becoming a relapse:

How I will get support to handle the relapse?

The next day . . .

High-Risk Situations for the Week

Work with your therapist to identify at least one high-risk situation coming up in the next week. Write down ideas about how to handle this situation on the High-Risk Situations worksheet. Use the back of your self-recording card to record how you actually handled the anticipated situation, and write down any unexpected high-risk situations that may have arisen during the week.

Homework

✎ Continue self-recording. Remember to use the back of your self-recording cards to write down the ways you handled your high-risk situations for the week.

✎ If not done in session, finish your plan for handling slips and relapses.

✎ Review the information in this chapter.

High-Risk Situations

What high-risk situations do you think you may experience this week?

Situation 1:
How can you handle this situation?

a. _____

b. _____

c. _____

d. _____

Situation 2:
How can you handle this situation?

a. _____

b. _____

c. _____

d. _____

Situation 3:
How can you handle this situation?

a. _____

b. _____

c. _____

d. _____

Situation 4:
How can you handle this situation?

a. _____

b. _____

c. _____

d. _____

Chapter 12

Session 12: Review / Relapse Prevention Part IV: Maintenance Planning and Relapse Contract

Goals

■ To identify the skills you will continue to use to maintain your progress in the future

■ To create and sign a relapse contract

Graphing Progress

In session, you will review the week with your therapist and together update your Alcohol Use and Urges Graph in Chapter 2 using the information from your most recently completed self-recording cards. You should see a marked decrease in your urges to drink alcohol, compared to when you first started this program. Take some time to look at the graph and think about all that you've done to create these changes. Think about how hard it was in those first few weeks and how you don't want to start drinking and have to go through all that again.

The End of Treatment

This week marks the end of the program and your final session with your therapist. The goal of this session is to remind you that you now have the skills to remain abstinent. You have learned a set of skills that can be applied in everyday life to deal with high-risk situations. The relapse-prevention techniques you have been taught will help you maintain gains made during treatment. Control of your life is now back in your own hands.

Think about the skills you have learned in this program:

Alcohol-Related Skills

1. Understanding alcohol in a different way (standard drinks, blood alcohol level, as a toxin that affects you medically, etc.)

2. Self-recording cravings and drinking, linking to triggers

3. Identifying and becoming more aware of triggers

4. Drinking behavior chains: thinking through the drink

5. Self-management planning to cope with triggers, including heavy drinkers in your social network

6. Self-control procedures using your thoughts: thinking about negative consequence of drinking, challenging and replacing positive thoughts about alcohol

7. Positive alternatives to drinking: using your former drinking time to do fun things without the use of alcohol and making sober life fun and satisfying

8. Drink-refusal skills

9. Relapse-prevention strategies: identifying seemingly irrelevant decisions, anticipating and planning for upcoming high-risk situations, identifying and managing warning signs for relapse, coping with slips or relapses

General Coping Skills

1. Understanding and coping with sadness and anxiety

2. Challenging and replacing negative thoughts to better control your emotions

3. Connecting with others

4. Assertiveness

5. Anger management

6. Problem solving

Identify the ones that have been most important to the changes you have made. Which skills will you continue to use in order to maintain progress now that treatment is ending? Write them down in the space provided.

1. _____

2. _____

3. _____

4. _____

5. _____

6. _____

Relapse Contract

Think about the things you are willing to do in order to prevent relapse. Write down your thoughts in the space provided and use them to create a relapse contract that you and your therapist can sign. A sample relapse contract is also provided to give you an idea of how to format your own contract.

What I will do to prevent relapse:

_____

_____

_____

_____

_____

Sample Relapse Contract

1. If I drink alcohol at all, in any amount, I will leave the situation as soon as possible. I will sit down the following day and review what to do in the event of a relapse. I will use my trigger sheets to figure out what happened. I will tell my partner (or best friend, sibling, etc.) and ask for his or her support.

2. If I drink again within a month, I will call my therapist with the goal of getting a referral to getting back into treatment, or coming back in for a "booster session."

3. If I drink even once in a binge (out of control) fashion, I will call, with the goal of getting back into treatment.

4. My goal is to remain abstinent for at least _____. At that time I will reevaluate this contract and write a new one.

_____   _____

Client Signature   Date

Wrap-Up

Congratulations on successfully completing this program! You have worked very hard and we hope that you have seen improvement in your drinking problem. Remember the keys to maintaining your success:

(1) Keep motivated by remembering the problems that drinking created and the good that has come from not drinking.

(2) Use the skills you've learned.

(3) Accept that change is difficult—not every day will be easy—and that the most successful people learn how to ride out the tough times.

(4) Find ways to enjoy your life each day.

(5) Know that there always is help available if you need it—don't be embarrassed to ask.

Appendix of Forms

Log of Anxiety Situations and Thoughts

Keep a log this week of situations or thoughts that make you feel depressed. Rate each one from 0 to 10.

Date	Time	Situation	Thought	Anxiety level 0–10

Log of Anxiety Situations and Thoughts

Keep a log this week of situations or thoughts that make you feel depressed. Rate each one from 0 to 10.

Date	Time	Situation	Thought	Anxiety level 0–10
——	——	——	————	——
——	——	——	————	——
——	——	——	————	——
——	——	——	————	——
——	——	——	————	——
——	——	——	————	——
——	——	——	————	——
——	——	——	————	——
——	——	——	————	——
——	——	——	————	——
——	——	——	————	——
——	——	——	————	——
——	——	——	————	——
——	——	——	————	——
——	——	——	————	——
——	——	——	————	——

Log of Depressing Situations and Thoughts

Keep a log this week of situations or thoughts that make you feel sad or depressed. Rate each one from 0 to 10. We'll go over it next week.

Date	Time	Situation	Thought	Depression level 0–10

Challenging Negative Thoughts

Think about a situation where you felt depressed or anxious.

_____

_____

_____

Now list the **negative thoughts** you had, along with the emotion that went with that thought. Next, write a thought(s) that challenges and replaces each negative thought.

Negative thought (emotion generated: _____)

_____

_____

Challenge and replace thought (emotion generated: _____)

_____

_____

Negative thought (emotion generated: _____)

_____

_____

Challenge and replace thought (emotion generated: _____)

_____

_____

Negative thought (emotion generated: _____)

_____

_____

Challenge and replace thought (emotion generated: _____)

_____

_____

Challenging Negative Thoughts

Think about a situation where you felt depressed or anxious.

_____

_____

_____

Now list the **negative thoughts** you had, along with the emotion that went with that thought. Next, write a thought(s) that challenges and replaces each negative thought.

Negative thought (emotion generated: _____)

_____

_____

Challenge and replace thought (emotion generated: _____)

_____

_____

Negative thought (emotion generated: _____)

_____

_____

Challenge and replace thought (emotion generated: _____)

_____

_____

Negative thought (emotion generated: _____)

_____

_____

Challenge and replace thought (emotion generated: _____)

_____

_____

Anger Behavior Chain

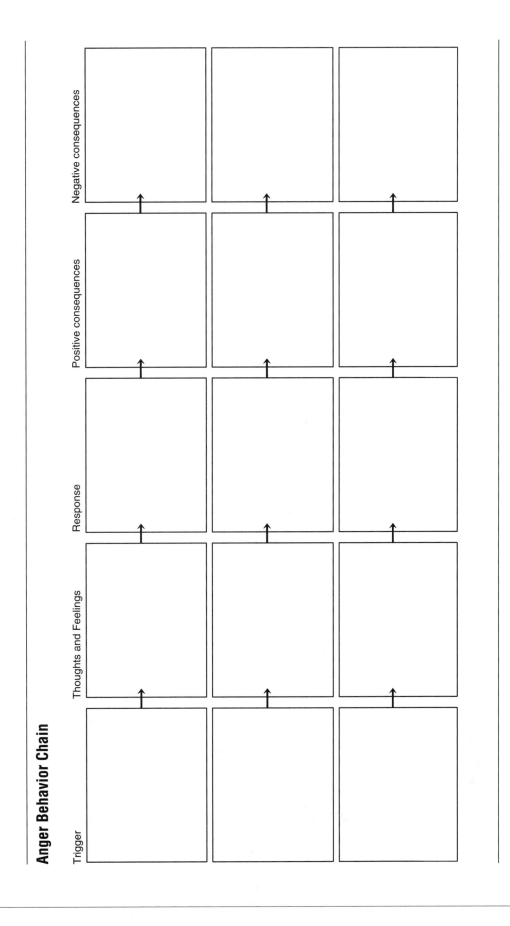

Trigger   Thoughts and Feelings   Response   Positive consequences   Negative consequences

Anger Behavior Chain

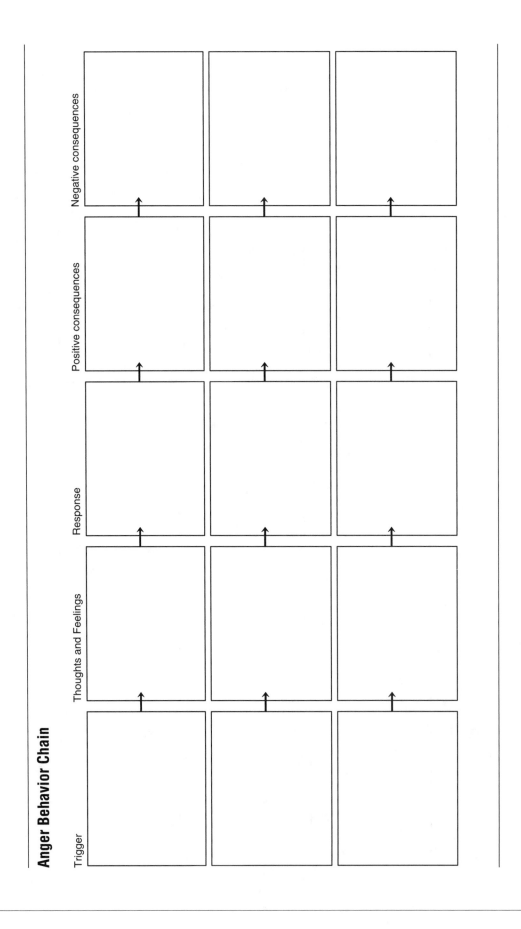

Problem-Solving Worksheet

Pick a problem that has come up in the course of treatment so far and practice solving it using the methods just described.

1. Gather Information: _____

2. Problem Definition: _____

3. Brainstorming for Solutions and Listing of Pros and Cons:

Solution	Pros (short and long term)	Cons (short and long term)
a.		
b.		
c.		
d.		
e.		

4. Pick solution(s): _____

5. Implement the solution for a period of time.

6. Reevaluate the solution—Did it work? _____

If not, do problem solving again.

Problem-Solving Worksheet

Pick a problem that has come up in the course of treatment so far and practice solving it using the methods just described.

1. Gather Information: _____

2. Problem Definition: _____

3. Brainstorming for Solutions and Listing of Pros and Cons:

Solution	Pros (short and long term)	Cons (short and long term)
a.		
b.		
c.		
d.		
e.		

4. Pick solution(s): _____

5. Implement the solution for a period of time.

6. Reevaluate the solution—Did it work? _____

   If not, do problem solving again.

Self-Recording Card

Daily monitoring   Date _____

Urges			Drinks				
Time	How strong? (1–7)	Trigger	Time	Type of drink	Amount (in ounces)	% Alcohol	Trigger

Self-Recording Card

Daily monitoring   Date _____

Urges

Time	How strong? (1–7)	Trigger

Drinks

Time	Type of drink	Amount (in ounces)	% Alcohol	Trigger

Self-Recording Card

Daily monitoring   Date _____

Urges			Drinks				
Time	How strong? (1–7)	Trigger	Time	Type of drink	Amount (in ounces)	% Alcohol	Trigger

Self-Recording Card

Daily monitoring

Date _____

Urges			Drinks				
Time	How strong? (1–7)	Trigger	Time	Type of drink	Amount (in ounces)	% Alcohol	Trigger

Self-Recording Card

Daily monitoring

Date _____

Urges			Drinks				
Time	How strong? (1–7)	Trigger	Time	Type of drink	Amount (in ounces)	% Alcohol	Trigger

Self-Recording Card

Daily monitoring   Date _____

Urges			Drinks				
Time	How strong? (1–7)	Trigger	Time	Type of drink	Amount (in ounces)	% Alcohol	Trigger

Self-Recording Card

Daily monitoring Date _____

Urges			Drinks				
Time	How strong? (1–7)	Trigger	Time	Type of drink	Amount (in ounces)	% Alcohol	Trigger

Self-Recording Card

Daily monitoring   Date _____

Urges

Time	How strong? (1–7)	Trigger

Drinks

Time	Type of drink	Amount (in ounces)	% Alcohol	Trigger

Self-Recording Card

Daily monitoring   Date _____

Urges			Drinks				
Time	How strong? (1–7)	Trigger	Time	Type of drink	Amount (in ounces)	% Alcohol	Trigger

Self-Recording Card

Daily monitoring

Date _____

Urges

Time	How strong? (1–7)	Trigger

Drinks

Time	Type of drink	Amount (in ounces)	% Alcohol	Trigger

Self-Recording Card

Daily monitoring

Date _____

Urges			Drinks				
Time	How strong? (1–7)	Trigger	Time	Type of drink	Amount (in ounces)	% Alcohol	Trigger

Self-Recording Card

Daily monitoring Date _____

Urges

Time	How strong? (1–7)	Trigger

Drinks

Time	Type of drink	Amount (in ounces)	% Alcohol	Trigger

Self-Recording Card

Daily monitoring

Date _____

Urges

Time	How strong? (1–7)	Trigger

Drinks

Time	Type of drink	Amount (in ounces)	% Alcohol	Trigger

Self-Recording Card

Daily monitoring   Date _____

Urges			Drinks				
Time	How strong? (1–7)	Trigger	Time	Type of drink	Amount (in ounces)	% Alcohol	Trigger

Self-Recording Card

Daily monitoring   Date _____

Urges			Drinks				
Time	How strong? (1–7)	Trigger	Time	Type of drink	Amount (in ounces)	% Alcohol	Trigger

Self-Recording Card

Daily monitoring

Date _____

Urges

Time	How strong? (1–7)	Trigger

Drinks

Time	Type of drink	Amount (in ounces)	% Alcohol	Trigger